Talk Like It Matters

Talk Like It Matters

A GUIDE TO GREAT CONVERSATIONS

Keith Allbritten

© 2025 by Keith Allbritten

All rights reserved.

This book or any portion thereof may not be reproduced or used in any manner whatsoever without the express written permission of the publisher except for the use of brief quotations in a book review.

ISBN: 979-8-9938701-0-6 (Paperback)
ISBN: 979-8-9938701-1-3 (Ebook)

Contents

Acknowledgments vii
Introduction ix

Chapter 1   It's Rare and Memorable 1
Chapter 2   We Long for Genuine Conversation 17
Chapter 3   The Mindshift 33
Chapter 4   What Would I See? 63
Chapter 5   Environment and Body Language 73
Chapter 6   The Words You Use 89
Chapter 7   The Genius Is in the Question 121
Chapter 8   Emotions 131

Conclusion: You Got This! 145
Author Biography 147

Acknowledgments

To all my coaching clients, workshop cohorts, and the outstanding team at Solutions 21, thank you. I've learned so much from each of you during our connections. A special shout-out to Mike P., a great friend and wisdom partner—I love talking with him because he's so full of insight. Thanks to my mom; I probably inherited her listening genes. Additional thanks to my sister—our long, insightful conversations sparked deep thoughts that helped me work through some of this material. Thanks also to Miranda Dunning, my editor. Her inputs were timely and spot on. Thanks for helping me get this project to the finish line.

Finally, I dedicate this book to my wonderful wife, Lisa, a critical thinking partner who helped me process these concepts as they entered my life. I couldn't have done it without her.

Introduction

---〰︎---

HERE'S THE THING: WE TRULY HAVE NO IDEA HOW MUCH WE NEED EACH OTHER

As I neared military retirement as a Wing Commander, I relinquished my position during a Change of Command ceremony to transition the Wing from one senior leader to another. It's a formal event, rooted in military tradition, where 1,100 Airmen of the Wing stand in formation. The Wing guidon (flag) is handed from the outgoing Commander to the incoming Commander, signifying the handoff of authority and responsibility. Since I was the outgoing Commander, I left the ceremony quietly. I didn't want to divert any attention away from the new Commander. My time had ended; this was his day.

As I was leaving, a friend approached and shook my hand. We were casual friends and had worked together for many years, although not closely. He told me an incredible story about one shotgun shell in his garage—one that had his name on it. The story weighed on me; it showed me the power and impact of a single, intentional conversation that changed the trajectory of a life and a family.

About seven years earlier, the Wing in Nashville made a significant mission transition. Without getting too deep in the weeds, it was like changing a blue-collar car manufacturing plant into a place where we wrote software code. Very few skill sets were similar, and about 80 percent of the Wing personnel were retrained into completely different career fields.

There was a sea of change during that time, and a lot of angst in the air. There were people issues everywhere, and they were all different—each requiring unique solutions. Let's just say there was a lot going on.

I was the Vice Commander (the number two person) and right in the middle of most all of it.

One of those guys in career transition had been a Guardsman for much of his life. He was close to retirement but not close enough, so he retrained to learn a new job. However, the transition had been hard for many people, and it was hard for him. He wasn't fitting into his role as well as he wanted and was struggling to meet the requirements. Change is hard. We'd casually talked a few times, and I knew he was struggling, but I didn't have any idea how much.

As I was walking around the base one afternoon, I happened to run into him. He was working late, as I was, so it was just the two of us. I stopped to talk for what I thought would be a few minutes, but those few minutes turned into an hour or so. We talked through his struggles, and I did a lot of listening. I don't remember everything, but I told him I would investigate his situation. I assured him we'd figure it out and find the right place for him until retirement. He was a great Airman, a hard worker, and competent. He had also given a lot for his country, and I wanted to honor that commitment for the last few years of his career. Besides that, we needed his expertise.

Over the next week or so, I made a few phone calls and found another role better suited for him. He performed well in that new role for the last few years of his career and retired after many years of commendable service. He had served faithfully and honorably, and our nation was better because of it. I didn't see him after he retired, but he came to the Change of Command ceremony five years later. That's where we pick up the story.

As we stood together that day, he asked if I remembered our conversation from back when he was struggling. Yes, I did, but not as well as he did. He told me he'd been only days away from using that shotgun shell when we had our conversation. The career transition had been hard, and he didn't know how he was going to make it. But our conversation had changed his mind. That conversation turned a light on at the end of the tunnel, and he didn't follow through with his plan.

Introduction

That conversation hit me hard. I don't tell that story to many people. Honestly, I'm not sure I've told it to anyone outside my family until writing about it now. I don't tell it so you'll think I always got it right, because I haven't. I've often wished for a mulligan to try again. But it shows the power of listening. I stopped, actively listened, and told him everything would be all right... and it made a difference. It made *all* the difference.

At the time, I didn't know if there was anything I could do for him. I didn't promise him anything that day, but I told him we would figure out a way forward. Thank goodness I stopped to talk with him. He was a great guy, and I'm glad it worked out.

We don't always get to see the impact of our words or our actions. That day, I was fortunate enough to see how powerful it can be when someone is fully seen and fully heard. So many things lined up for us that day. I knew something was troubling him. I could see it in his face, so I made time right then. I'm not saying every conversation you'll have will be as life altering as that one, but sometimes we don't know how important our conversations are. We truly have no idea how much we need each other.

WE HOLD THINGS CLOSE TO THE CHEST

Most of us don't share our true feelings in relationships. We don't realize how important it is to our well-being. We're also not very good about getting together one on one with our friends. Life gets in our way. It's a combination of not being appropriately vulnerable or purposefully intentional.

What's at risk in these missed connections? What's at stake? What happens when we don't get real with anyone? Loneliness is everywhere. On one hand, our digital society has enabled more connection than ever. We can communicate across multiple modes, day or night. We don't go anywhere without our phones; in fact, most of us feel lost without them! On the other hand, isolation and depression are on the rise. Despite numerous friends and connections, we lack genuine relationships—not just social media ties. There's a massive difference, and we all know it in our heart of hearts. We're leaving a lot on the table.

We don't talk like we used to

Many things that make conversation and connection successful aren't intuitive. Having a great conversation isn't as easy as it used to be because we don't talk like we used to: society has changed. Too many things are grasping for—and demanding—our attention. Constant connectivity on our phones has distanced us from one another. Instead of conversation, we doomscroll silently. I've heard it said that today's mobile phone is a weapon of mass distraction. We've forgotten how to talk.

Is it any wonder we're distracted? Any question we have can be answered at our fingertips. We evaluate every product by its reviews, research to find that best product of the moment, do *more* research to find the best price to get it here tomorrow—or even two hours from now. The next day, the process begins again with the next thing we can't survive without. Social media consumption and gaming up are claiming our hobbies, our free time, and our future. All these activities and efforts have led to atrophied conversational skills.

We all have lots of internet friends, but who's going to carry the other end of my couch on moving day? Who will be present when I'm struggling in my relationships? Who will be at the funeral home with me? To have a true friend—an in-person friend—you must be a friend when it counts.

How do we reclaim the ground we've lost?

How do we get it all back? It may seem like a monumental task, but I'll simply repeat some great advice I got from a former boss many years ago. You may have heard it too.

How do we eat an elephant? One bite at a time.

Let's take one small step at a time. Rome wasn't built in a day. Let's adopt some new moves to reclaim the ground we've given up. Let's reframe what conversation and connection really look like. It's not letters on a

Introduction

screen, or a text, or a chat, or an email. We know that communication comprises words, tone, and body language. All the asynchronous modes of communication are missing tone and body language—key parts of connection. Let's bring them back.

F2F

The highest and best option: Get face to face. It's a commitment, I know. In a text, I can ghost someone when the conversation gets uncomfortable. I can compose the perfect response because I can take all the time I want; I don't even have to get up off the couch. Where's the thrill in that? With great risk comes great reward. Nothing ventured, nothing gained. Can you even compare a video of a hike through the Grand Canyon with hiking it yourself? A text-to-real-conversation comparison is the same: they're not even in the same ballpark.

I'll also cover connecting virtually. It can be done effectively. Whether in person or virtual, we have the same goals, but we execute them differently.

Why would you want deeper, more meaningful connections?

We're all living life with lots of acquaintances but few true friends. Few people, if any, truly know you. Most of the time, we don't get real with anyone. So we don't really, truly know anyone. There must be more to life. We want to be seen and heard. Life is so quiet and shallow when you never get real.

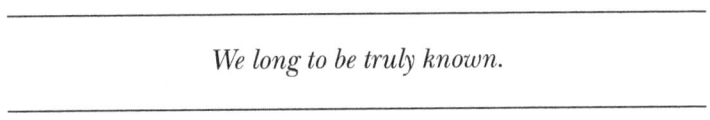

We long to be truly known.

There's so much more to life, and I want that for you. It takes effort, but it's worth it. The richness of life isn't found on your phone or a screen but in deep conversation and enduring, engaging friendships. These connections create bonds that carry us through the inevitable challenging days.

Deep down, you know this is true. These words resonate because they reach a part of us often overlooked in today's busy world.

The elephant isn't that big

The good thing is there's nothing mysterious about creating great connection. None of this is rocket science. There will be no Nobel Prizes or Pulitzers in my future. However, I'm giving you practical steps you can implement immediately. These are the tools of great conversation and connection.

I've spent thirty years as a military officer and leader. In that time, I've conducted over a thousand job interviews (yes, one thousand!). I've also facilitated hundreds of workshops and coached hundreds of people. This book is the culmination of all those experiences, the things I've stumbled into and discovered along the way, nuggets that were hidden in plain sight.

Let's look with different eyeballs

At one point in my military career, I took a vulnerability assessment course. It taught me to look for flaws and cracks in security protocols. Afterward, I saw security vulnerabilities everywhere: at the airport, at my kids' school, everywhere I went. It put different eyeballs in my head, and I started seeing things I'd never seen before. This book will put different eyeballs in your head that will enable you to see conversations differently. You'll make deeper connections. You'll cultivate close, dear relationships with your friends on a deeper level than ever before.

Get ready to get real

You'll have to be authentic. This book isn't a transactional checklist of behaviors to adopt. If you're not authentic, the other person will spot it. Remember the unflattering words of Jerry Seinfeld about another comedian: "He's nothing but a phony." You might fool a few folks here and there in the short term, but most people will see through it. That fake move will destroy any chance you have for real connection—maybe for good. Most folks don't forget hypocrisy.

Introduction

Bottom line: If your heart isn't in it, don't try it. Put this book aside until you're ready. Go get a latte and check the markets.

It's some science ... but mostly art

Connection is more art than science, with intentionality rolled in. It's knowing when to be silent and how to listen, or when to speak and what to say.

I also realize that not everything will work for everyone. Great relationships rarely have universal rules. Some of the tools and concepts will resonate, but some won't. You must decide what works best for you. But if you take these chapters to heart, you'll increase your connection with those around you. It could be with friends, coworkers, relatives, in-laws, or outlaws. You may think they won't work for you, but I encourage you to give it a go. People see your honest efforts, even fumbling efforts, and they'll be richly rewarded. Having better connections will transform your relationships.

Never let the fear of striking out get in your way. In 1935, Babe Ruth held the MLB record for the most strikeouts. This was a time when strikeouts were unfavorable, but he was aggressive—which led to him becoming the home run king. By the way, he held that strikeout record until 1964. Guess who took the record from him? Mickey Mantle. Two of the all-time greats, swinging for the fence.

Begin with this

When you're ready to really talk with people, to make that connection, you're beginning a journey with limits only you can set. There's no suitcase, no change of clothes required—just a mustard seed of genuine desire to better connect with people in your world. As you read, begin with the idea of putting yourself aside ... put the other first. If you can't do this, you won't be as effective as you could be.

Put yourself aside. Put the other first.

While writing this book, I conducted a reasonable amount of research, but I'm not a scientist. My conclusions are based on countless conversations, comments during workshops, small group discussions, coaching sessions, feedback over the years, and anecdotal comments and experiences. It all adds up to lessons in the school of life. There are some hard knocks and painful lessons in here, and I have a few bruises that remain discolored. And I have some regret that lingers. But you'll also read about a few victories. Those are what keep us going.

> *There are a thousand thoughts lying within a man that*
> *he does not know until he takes up the pen to write.*
> —William Makepeace Thackeray

The book is conversational and informal. If I were a scientist, a researcher, or an academic, this book might be different. But I'm a blue-collar guy and a product of the public school system. My dad was a fireman and painter, and my stepdad was a bricklayer; I worked for both growing up. I worked in the fields as a farmer's hand during the summer and was a factory worker on the midnight shift, making toys for Fisher-Price. Other jobs included high school math teacher, carpenter's apprentice, and beer joint bartender. All this was before I joined the US Air Force, serving all over the world with all kinds of folks.

What I do know is how to talk to people, to relate to them, how to connect. Early in my coaching career, I was having a Zoom conversation with a client—it was our first meeting. We'd been going for about forty-five minutes when he said to me, "You know about as much about me as my drinking buddy Sam." Right then, I thought, I've succeeded. When I heard that, I knew I'd made the connection. That was my goal. I don't care so much about letters after my name, and I don't care if I impress people or not—I just want to relate to people.

I once read that a truly exceptional naval captain's greatest strengths were understanding people and showing kindness. This is what I would hope to outline to you. The knowledge of human nature is so useful. Understanding one another, along with a little spoonful of kindness, will dramatically enhance our connections.

SWING FOR THE FENCE

Right away, start putting these things into action. As a military aviator I've always said that there's no substitute for seat time. Put in the reps. Keep at it, and they'll work for you.

You can't accelerate experience; you have to live through it.

I encourage you to swing for the fence. Play ball like Babe and Mickey. Now I know you can't swing at every pitch. Some of them are way outside the strike zone. But when the ball *is* in the strike zone, swing for it. You'll never even get a hit, much less a home run, if you don't swing.

Even if you believe you're a terrible listener, put your best effort into it and see what happens. It's like traveling to another country and trying to speak their language. Your sincere (albeit clumsy) attempt is attractive and attractional. It warms the other to you. They can tell you're trying, and even when you mess it up, they appreciate it. You can see their smile, and you know you're not getting it quite right, but the shared experience creates magic and connection. The same thing happens with listening.

I'm still working on it. There are days where I'm not very good at this. I'm not always as intentional as I would like to be, and sometimes my situational awareness is subpar. But I'm on the journey, too, and these tools have helped me get further down the road.

I'll keep stepping up to the plate and swinging. Nothing says *missed opportunity* like watching the ball come across in the zone while the bat is resting on the batter's shoulder.

You'll do all right. Trust me.

I'll see you at the plate.

CHAPTER 1

It's Rare and Memorable

―∽―

*Listening is a magnetic and strange thing, a creative force.
The friends who listen to us are the ones we move toward.*
—Karl Menninger

As the Wing Commander of a US Air Force base, I was busy. I led 1,100 Airmen in widely differing disciplines across five major divisions. As the senior officer on the installation, I was responsible for a myriad of moving parts, and a lot was often riding on the line.

To help keep things moving, I had a personal assistant who owned my calendar and was able to schedule meetings on my behalf. One day I noticed a recent hire in a key role wanted to sit down with me for a few minutes so we could get to know each other.

Honestly, the boldness of a move like that impressed me. I don't see that very often; there were two layers of supervision between us in the organizational chart. When the time came, we had a great conversation. After announcing my military retirement a few years later, that person called to offer his congratulations. We talked for a few minutes about the normal things you would expect, but then he got real with me.

"Do you remember the first time I came to see you?"

"Of course I do," I said.

"When I came by that day, we spent an hour and a half together. The whole time we were together, you never looked at your phone, you never looked at your watch, and you didn't take any calls. I knew you were a busy guy with a lot going on, but you took the time to spend with me that day. That's when I knew you cared."

After all that time, he remembered the time I invested in him. It stuck with him. He remembered when he was the most important thing in someone else's life. Through all my interactions with people, I didn't always get it right—but that day I did.

Another part of my role was serving as the senior civilian employee on the installation. It was complicated being both the senior military and civilian authority. As the civilian authority, I dealt with the union, executed the budget, developed leaders, and was the final approval authority for disciplinary action. It was an interesting role, and I learned a lot about people.

At one point, I had a civilian employee who wanted to discuss his work schedule. He was asking for an accommodation I most likely wouldn't be able to approve. Two levels of supervisors before me had already denied his request. He asked for my review—the final level. I agreed to meet with him if he also brought his supervisor.

We met and talked for about twenty minutes. Sure enough, I couldn't do what he wanted me to do. As he was leaving, he said, "Thank you. You've given me more time and attention than the previous two people put together. I didn't think you'd be able to do anything, but I appreciate you listening."

Until we talked, he hadn't been fully heard, and he knew it. The outcome didn't change after our discussion, but something else did. Once I fully listened to him, he was okay with the decision.

I've heard this sentiment expressed repeatedly: people just want to be seen; they want to be heard. It's not too much to ask, but it's rare and memorable when it happens. Sometimes people just want an opportunity to tell their story to the Man (or Woman). They want that person to really listen, and they want to be truly heard.

Those friends who truly listen stand head and shoulders above the crowd because they make us feel interesting. They really hear us, and that makes the experience unique.

WE ARE TERRIBLE LISTENERS

Most people aren't very good at listening. Shocking, I know. We've all experienced it firsthand. If we're brutally honest with ourselves, we'd say we've been poor listeners to others. Society today isn't helping: we're always connected and getting more distracted every day.

Active listening is a challenge. Two-thirds of global professionals say that listening has become significantly more difficult in today's digital workplace.[1] It's also affecting people's direct reports. Over 70 percent of employees have been negatively affected by poor listening skills.[2]

THE WORST LISTENERS DON'T HAVE A CLUE

Most people are unaware that they're bad listeners. One study looked specifically at the subgroup of managers rated worst in listening effectiveness.[3] When asked to rate themselves, 94 percent rated themselves as good or very good listeners. How about that for self-awareness. In my humble opinion, there's generally a dramatic gap between how well we *think* we listen and how well we *actually* listen.

This blind spot is known as the Dunning-Kruger effect: it's when a person's lack of knowledge and skill in a certain area causes them to overestimate their own competence. Because these managers think they're good at listening, they don't even think to work on it.

The great enemy of communication is the illusion of it.
We have talked enough; but we have not listened.
—W. H. Whyte

---

[1] Accenture, 2014.
[2] Talbot, 2023.
[3] Brownell, 1990.

Talk Like It Matters

You can't be transactional

A while back, I was with two new friends—I'll call them Listening Larry and Tone Deaf Tommy—in a nearby town doing volunteer work for the morning. Tone Deaf Tommy was at the wheel, Listening Larry was riding shotgun, and I was in the back seat.

Listening Larry was talking about his family when he dropped a bombshell. His exact words were, "My dad's grandparents were Jewish, and they were killed in the Holocaust."

Wow. That conversation got real, real quick.

While I was still processing that, an audible "Wow" having barely escaped my lips, Tone Deaf Tommy calmly spoke up, pointing his finger over to the right. "Up here is a restaurant that my wife and I used to go to, but I think it's gone out of business."

I was utterly shocked. I was simultaneously trying to process the impact of the Holocaust on a family while marveling at Tone Deaf Tommy's comment. That bombshell Holocaust statement was still hanging thick in the air when Tommy made the restaurant comment. He was so absorbed in himself that Listening Larry's statement didn't even register. It was as if the words had never been said.

The whole time we were out, Tone Deaf Tommy's conversations were transactional and almost exclusively about him. A few minutes later, I told a very moving, significant personal story that landed with Listening Larry, but Tone Deaf Tommy never made a sound—not even a grunt.

Larry and I had a really good conversation. He was engaging, reaching in at the right moments, appropriately digging deep, asking great questions about life and family. Meaningful conversations like this form the foundation of a great connection.

Meanwhile, Tommy was right there in the car with us, but never looked beyond himself. He never caught on. He was unable or unwilling to move away from himself. I'm not sure he got past all the unimportant, surface details of his life that were simply small talk to fill the space. Tone Deaf Tommy's poor conversational skills caused him to leave a lot on the table.

It's easy to see if you're looking for it

You can see poor listening in action during a group conversation. The dynamics are interesting to watch. You'll see listeners and talkers, and others somewhere in between.

It gets interesting when you get two talkers together. You'll see one talker telling a story while the other talker is jockeying for position. He's looking for that millisecond break to jump in and tell his story. As soon as talker number one gets to any point that resembles a break in the action—maybe they slow down to take a breath—talker number two jumps in with a version of, "Yeah, that's interesting, but let me tell you what happened to me the other day." You know what I'm talking about. You've seen it. Talker number two already knows what they're going to say; they're just waiting for the chance to say it.

Listening is an art—it's not just waiting to talk.

Why is it so hard to listen well?

We're not great at listening. Most of us are thinking about what happened yesterday, what's for lunch, or what we'll say when the other person stops talking. Our minds drift.

One of my workshop participants described this well: "Sometimes when I'm listening to conversations, I check out and my mind wanders. It's not intentional, but it happens." It's insidious—it sneaks up on us. Why?

We can think and process conversation faster than people speak.

Focused listening is a challenge because we can think and process words faster than people speak; our brains are that powerful. The average speaking rate for most people is between 135 and 175 words per minute[4]; however, the brain can process speech at up to twice that rate.[5] If you're like me, you speed up your podcasts to get through them faster. Most of the time, I'm listening at one and a half times and catching every word.

WE'VE GOT UNUSED COGNITIVE BANDWIDTH

Our brains are powerful enough to both fully listen to what someone is saying and think of other things while they're talking. We've got unused cognitive bandwidth—in other words, there's margin available in our minds. There's room in the inn. I've got more cards to play, and I'm just waiting for the chance to roll out the trump card as soon as you're done talking.

We daydream or think of many other things. The brain sees the available margin and begins to multitask. We've all heard that multitasking doesn't work; it brings distraction, and we lose focus. I can get distracted listening to an auctioneer—and you know how fast they talk!

We see distracted driving all the time because driving doesn't take all our brainpower. How many of us have driven from one place to another yet can't remember anything along the way? That's an indication of how little cognitive bandwidth it takes.

Pair that with our efficiency-driven world and it's a recipe for distraction. I've seen women on the interstate putting on makeup in the rearview mirror as they drive to work. I also see it at the barbershop—there's a TV right in front of the chair, tuned to the sports channel. Guys can't even sit and get a haircut for twenty minutes without wanting to keep their brains busy.

It's not getting any better. Our world is always on, telling us to always be fully engaged in something. Distraction and multitasking are byproducts, and defeating those two giants will be a lifelong endeavor. It might get easier, but it'll never be easy.

So we understand why our minds wander. We see why we're so easily

---

[4] Talbot, 2023.

[5] Raynor and Clifton, 2009.

distracted. This unused cognitive bandwidth creates a perfect storm for poor listening; it makes it too easy to think of other things instead of focusing on what you're saying to me right now.

When our minds wander, it shows. Quite often, the other person can see it when it happens. It may be hard for them to put their finger on what tipped them off, but they know. They figure it out. When you see someone driving in front of you and they're all over the road, you know they're distracted. It shows. And we see the same thing in our conversations with others.

This distractive cognitive function can build up in a conversation. Think of a time in conversation when you remembered a task you needed to do; you may have forgotten it twice already. You can't forget it again! You focus on it and repeat it to yourself again, trying to remember it. Your mind is consumed with it. Finally, you get to a place where you can write it on a piece of paper and put that paper in your pocket.

Guess what? You were a terrible listener that whole time. Often in conversation, we're just not fully there. Our challenge is to be fully present in the moment.

Consider my friend Nate

Let's contrast that with my friend Nate. He's a wonderful person, and I enjoy being around him. A big part of my feelings for Nate is centered on one of his mantras: "Wherever you are, be all there."

When I'm talking to Nate, I have his full attention. It's as if I'm the only person in the universe. Let me repeat that: the only person in the universe. He's fully present and focused on me.

How do I know? Body language, the words he uses, and eye contact, to name a few. All of it becomes a wonderful experience. I've talked to others about Nate, and they have the same feelings; they smile when his name comes up.

Nate literally stops his life when he's talking with someone. It couldn't be more obvious if he wore a shirt that said "I'm here for you."

You know people like Nate. If you don't, you should. They're a pleasure to be around. If you do, I'll bet you don't know many—they're few and far between. Nate is 100 percent present. He's along for the ride, wherever it goes; it doesn't matter to him. No agenda except me. It's a beautiful thing. Nate is intentional in his conversations; he's focused on the other, and this focus is where the magic is. That's why he's so good at it. There's a good intensity there.

THINK ABOUT LISTENING

Have you ever spent much time thinking about listening? Of the people I've talked to, very few have given it much thought. When asked to describe active listening, most people can tell you what it means. The question is, have they practiced it? Are they intentional about it, or have they self-evaluated? We've talked about it as a passing point of conversation, but we've never stopped to consider how we can improve.

This is hard work at first; it takes effort that most people don't consciously consider. It's like leadership. Many people think becoming a great leader is reserved for a select few born with special skills—maybe George S. Patton or Abraham Lincoln or someone like that. Leadership is a skill that can be developed with intention and self-reflection.

Listening is the same way. If you think about, read about, study, practice, and reflect on listening, before long, you'll have become a better listener. You'll be the one people want to talk to. People will say, "You know about as much about me as my drinking buddy Sam." With a little effort and intention, you'll wake up one day and be the person you wanted to be when you started reading this book.

Listening is the currency of connection; there's no substitute.

Think of that person you know is a great listener. It's someone you always look forward to talking with because they make you feel special. Great conversationalists are great listeners. By letting these chapters and discussions sink in, you can become that person. You'll become the one people talk to—and I mean *really* talk to. When you start listening like this, you may be the only person in their life who listens this way.

WE'RE SO CONNECTED, BUT WE'RE NOT ACTUALLY CLOSE TO ANYONE

In our modern society, we don't verbally communicate as much as we used to. Two hundred years ago, we communicated with newspapers, letters, and word of mouth. These days, it would be hard to list all our synchronous and asynchronous ways of communicating: posts, comments, chats, texts, social media, and so on.

Our ways of connecting have become as diverse as humanity, yet so many people still aren't close to anyone. This lack of authentic connection has even led to the growth of a new career field: professional cuddlers. Yes, truth is indeed stranger than fiction.

According to a 2019 article in *Experience Magazine*, cuddlers physically connect with others in a nonsexual way to provide nurturing, platonic touch in a therapeutic setting. A quick internet search, and you can find all kinds of info about cuddlers—even a website to find one near you. Why would we need this? Loneliness is an epidemic that keeps growing. We're wired for connection. In the absence of it, we will find other ways to connect, even if we have to pay for it.

TRUE FRIENDSHIPS ARE FEW AND FAR BETWEEN

So many people have so few people to talk to. Most people just need someone to really listen—to be the center of your life for only a few minutes. That's true friendship. They don't want easy, unsolicited advice; they just want you to listen patiently. They want presence.

My experience is that most are never transparent with anyone. The few who do get real with others can count those friends on just a few fingers. Heck, we're not even fully transparent with ourselves! We long to be known and to fully know others, yet we hide behind a façade of "I'm fine."

Most people have no one they can get real with.

We rush through life in such a hurry that we don't realize the things that are truly important: real friends, real connection. These things can't be found or bought; they must be nurtured and cultivated.

I read the same sentiment in a hundred-year-old essay:

> Friends, real friends, are rare in the individual life. We cannot have many of them. They do not come in bunches like bananas. They are never found ready-made at all. They are formed by weathering the same gales of fate together, by standing the heat of conflict together, by kinship of mind and heart, by common interest in a common ideal, by basic understanding, mutual dependence, thorough respect, and loyalty that grows stronger as need grows greater. Acquaintances we may have many, but acquaintanceship is merely the grapes of possibility from which the rich wine of friendship is aged and mellowed.[6]

Aged and mellowed. Let that sink in for a minute. Think of your true friends. Most likely, those friendships could be described as aged and mellowed.

GET IN THE DEEP END

Think of conversation as a swimming pool. There's no growth in talk on the surface. I want to get in the deep end. You'll hear me repeat this because it's so fundamental to connection. The quicker you can get into a meaningful conversation, the faster your connection will grow.

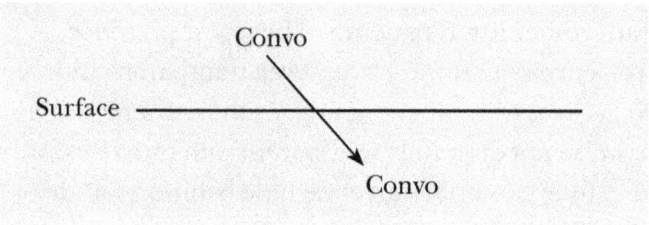

---

[6] Jordan, *The Crown of Individuality*

When you begin to have conversations like this, your connections will immediately benefit. Small talk is often the social lubricant of our engagements, so it's okay to start there. It gets conversations going. But as smoothly and quickly as you can, move past small talk and get in the deep water. For our first conversation, that may be a bit aggressive, but you get the idea. Maybe the first time we talk, I'm not going to get too deep. But after a while, I'll try it out and see what happens.

What are those things in the deep water? Topics like values, beliefs, and experiences. These topics are emotionally connected to the core of who we are and how we see the world.

Some people aren't deep thinkers. They don't want to get below the surface. Maybe their family upbringing was tough. Maybe it hurts too much to think deeply. Maybe it's a tough season for them. All that's okay. But sometimes you run into someone who wants to go deeper—I want you to be ready for that.

Why do people not get in the deep end of the pool more often? One answer may be in a study I heard about on a *Hidden Brain* podcast in 2024. Researchers conducted an experiment in which they called participants into a room and gave them a choice of two tasks for the next twenty minutes: sit alone with their thoughts or sort 1,500 red and blue pencils into two piles (red pencils and blue pencils). Surprisingly—or maybe not—people overwhelmingly chose to sort pencils. The study found that people will go to great lengths to avoid silently spending time alone with their thoughts. Maybe this same aversion to thinking deeply keeps people out of the deep end of the pool. It's certainly less mentally taxing to talk about the local sports team and the weather.

Even if it does come together, remember that most people just want to sort pencils. They want to stay on the surface with their discussion. It's easier and safer up there. Many people just avoid going there—but life gets shallow when you don't, no pun intended. You leave a lot on the table.

The Johari window gets us in the deep end

In 1955, psychologists Joseph Luft and Harry Ingham came up with a psychological model called the Johari window that explains why knowing people better helps with connection. I would've come up with a snappier name, but that's just me.

It's best explained with a diagram that looks like a four-paned window.

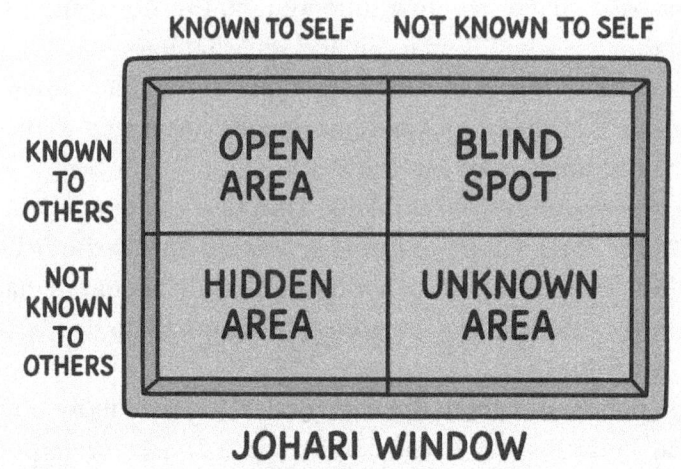

- The Open Area contains information known to both people—it's things like what color shirt I'm wearing. We both know this info.
- The Blind Spot contains things you know about me but I don't know about myself. When I'm deep in thought, I make a face that looks like I'm angry, but I don't know that.
- The Hidden Area contains things I know about myself that you don't know. Maybe I appear like I've got it all together, but I really don't feel that way most of the time. I keep this hidden from the world.
- The Unknown Area contains information unknown to both of us.

The magic happens when we move information from the Blind Spot and Hidden Area into the Open Area. As we share about ourselves and gain feedback, we begin to build trust and connection. The more we know about each other, the closer we become. When I share my self-doubt with you, it moves out of the Hidden Area and into the Open Area, and we grow closer together. When you tell me about the angry face that shows up when I'm deep in thought, that bit of knowledge moves from the Blind Spot into the Open Area, and we grow closer together.

The more you know about someone, the better connected you are. One of my goals when I begin a relationship is to move as much information as I can into the Open Area. It could be information about me or you, but that's my goal. This increases connection.

The more I get to know someone, the better I understand them.
—Workshop participant

I was in a small group when one person shared his struggles with his brother, which prompted someone else to share about similar struggles with his own brother. This kind of sharing creates a stronger, deeper connection.

One topic that always comes up is the idea of oversharing, or when we move inappropriate things into the Open Area. Oversharing is uncomfortable for everyone and is something to avoid. But there's a downside to the flip side: undersharing. If you hardly talk about yourself, you're not moving things into the Open Area. There's a sweet spot somewhere—take a little risk and try to find it.

CONNECTION HAPPENS WHEN YOU GET TO KNOW SOMEONE
Johari, simply put: Connection happens when you get to know someone. The better you get to know them, the better the connection. One of the ways to get to know someone better is to get into the deep end of the pool. However, many of our conversations are small talk about

the weather or who's playing college football this weekend; this often doesn't move any significant information into the Open Area.

YOU'RE THE ONLY PERSON WHO KNOWS THIS

When I'm talking with people, they tell me things they rarely tell others. Just before the telling, they say things like, "You're the only person I'll tell this to," or "Fewer than five people know this," or "I don't have good conversations like this with anyone." They say these things to me because I'm really listening and being curious. Those qualities will help you thrive in an underpopulated field of listeners.

When we can't truly share our unvarnished feelings with someone—when no one really hears us—it leaves us unfulfilled. We've all felt this.

I asked a client one day what was most helpful about our connection. He answered, "Simply having someone's full attention who's unbiased. Someone who is actively listening and can actually chime in with helpful thoughts. To slow down for a minute together. That's rare to come by." He's right. Our society doesn't encourage slowing down, but that's just what we need.

I have another good friend, Malcolm. At our very first meeting over coffee, he said something that has stuck with me: "I want to hear your cuts-and-bruises stories." In other words: Let's get real. Let's get in the deep end. Small talk—surface talk—doesn't get us where we want to go. It doesn't fill our deepest needs.

FRIENDSHIP AND CONNECTION ARE SPELLED T–I–M–E

How do we build those friendships? If you ask how to spell connection, most people will reply, "T–I–M–E." Every human understands how important time is. I can make more money, but when time is spent, it can't be replaced. It's not a renewable resource. When we give it to someone, it's a true gift.

Connection is one of those things that's hard to rush. It takes time. You can't get better conversation when you're in a hurry. There are ways to accelerate things, but generally speaking, you have to invest time in people to increase the connection. The day you plant the seed (first conversation) isn't the day you reap the harvest (follow-on connection).

I use the word *invest* very intentionally. Always think of it that way—never as an expense. An expense is transactional and has no return, whereas an investment pays dividends: it grows. Real connection is never transactional.

Friendship is cooked in a crockpot, not a microwave.

Great friendships must be patiently nurtured and cultivated. Friendships that receive the sunshine of our attention will grow; conversely, those in the shadows will fade and wither.

What do people regret at the end of life? Things and stuff are never in their answers, but deeper connections and friendships are. An *Old Colony Hospice* article from 2014 pondered end-of-life thoughts, noting that "there were many deep regrets about not giving friendships the time and effort that they deserved." This isn't a grand revelation to anyone, but we humans are so forgetful. We need to be reminded often.

I know what you're saying: I don't have that kind of time! I've got too much going on!

Funny thing is, we all have the same amount of time. There are twenty-four hours in a day for every person. It's not a resource issue we're talking about; it's a matter of prioritization and choices. We're simply not taking the time to invest in others, and the number and depth of our friendships prove this. The choices we make give us the output we have. We think we're too busy, but are we busy doing the right things?

To get a different answer, we must go upstream and change the input. Friendships are the same: to have deeper friendships, we must change our priorities.

I was in a leadership position, and a friend came to see me for some feedback. He didn't work directly for me, but we'd worked closely together in the recent past, and we were still good friends. He stopped by one afternoon, and I'll never forget his words: "I came to you because I knew you would tell me what I needed to hear." He knew I was a truth-teller, and he knew I would give him the time he needed. People appreciate honesty, especially when your words are weighty; it causes people to listen, to pay attention when you decide to speak.

For my friend, there were others in more appropriate positions to give him feedback, but he wasn't convinced that they would be honest with him. I understood why he came to see me. We talked for over two hours that afternoon. Thinking back on it, I'm certain I could have been gentler in my delivery. I had to tell him things he didn't really want to hear, but he came to me for truth, and he knew he would get it from me.

It's time for change

Whenever we recognize the need for change, the old proverb comes to mind: When is the best time to plant a tree? Twenty years ago. When is the second-best time to plant a tree? Today. Now is the time for action; today is the day for change.

I'll borrow a familiar financial term to describe it: asset allocation. Where we invest our money may differ, but it's a choice we make. Think of time in the same fashion. The asset allocation model will vary from person to person, but we all start with the same amount in our bucket.

Maybe it's time to change your asset allocation. A Nate is rare and memorable; I want that for you.

CHAPTER 2

We Long for Genuine Conversation

—∽—

We are hungry for a chance to talk.
—Margaret Wheatley

ONE OF MY BANKER FRIENDS told me an interesting story about a catfishing experience that happened at his bank. An elderly woman in her seventies came in to do a large-sum wire transfer, and that's when his Spidey sense started tingling: This looked suspicious.

We've all heard of catfishing: creating a fake persona to gain something from another person. As a banker, he's trained to spot fraudulent transactions; he knows the questions to ask to ensure his customers aren't being scammed. Unfortunately, once the transaction is complete, the money is usually unrecoverable. This situation got his attention.

His conversation began with a few probing questions. After determining that she had her full mental capacity, his next few questions were more direct. He quickly concluded she was probably being catfished. He gently brought up the idea that this could be a scam. At first, she denied the possibility, but after a few minutes she quietly nodded and agreed it was probably a scam.

Her next words were powerful: "I know this is probably fake, but I'm lonely and it fills a void in my life. He's saying what I need to hear." At the end of the day, it's her money. She knows what she's doing and is walking into it with eyes wide open. You might even say she's getting what she's paying for. Services rendered, invoice paid.

The conversation concluded, and she executed the wire transfer. To her, the money was worth it.

We are wired for connection. Things and stuff just don't do it for us.

Conversation, connection . . . these are the things that really matter. This woman was willing to pay for it and tell herself that it was okay. That's how badly we want it.

WE ENJOY GREAT CONVERSATION

I asked several people what makes a good conversationalist. The consistent answer was "People that get you to talk about yourself."

Anyone interested in how human nature works should read Dale Carnegie's book *How to Win Friends and Influence People*. It was written a long time ago, but as we know, people don't change. It's still relevant and recommended reading.

Carnegie tells a story of a botanist he talked to for several hours. He invested the time asking questions and listening. The botanist closed the evening by saying that Carnegie was "a most interesting conversationalist."[2] What's interesting is that Carnegie said little and listened much. That made all the difference. A good conversationalist is someone who keeps the other person talking and really listens when they do.

I think listening is all people really need.
—Workshop participant

There's an energy in the air when you're talking with the right person. They're asking about you, appropriately digging in with great questions and accompanying body language. It's palpable when you talk with someone who is truly interested and really listening. They're listening as if no one else is around. You appreciate it because it's certainly not commonplace. It's much better to be interested than interesting.

Active listening is a powerful move. An online research article at wordsrated.com mentioned that employee satisfaction increases by 30 percent after managers are trained in active listening. Higher employee satisfaction leads to higher retention rates. That's a good thing, because it's hard to find the right person in a tight labor market. Now that the average cost to hire a new employee is equal to their annual salary, it becomes even more powerful.

We were made for connection

We long for companionship and desire to be fully known by someone, warts and all. To quote from the bestselling book of all time, "It is not good for man to be alone" (Genesis 2:18). We want to be forgiven for who we were yesterday, accepted for who we are today, and encouraged in our journey of who we will fully become.

These are the things we share with each other in genuine conversation. People feel validated when you ask deep questions and really listen to their answers. Truth is, we need so many people in our lives to complete us, but many of us look around and find few (if any) people standing with us.

We long to get in the deep end of the pool, but we rarely do. Our values, beliefs, and experiences aren't things we talk about much.

---

*We long to be fully known, and we fear it
more than anything.*
—Chip Dodd

You're probably not surprised to learn that we're wired for connection. You knew it in your heart before you read it here.

MY FRIEND MIKE

Military commanders are responsible for the combat readiness of their troops. This includes discrete things like equipment, manpower, and training; readiness also includes other, less tangible things like mental readiness. My friend Mike is an award-winning counselor who worked tirelessly to ensure the mental readiness of the Airmen under my command.

Mike and I were in the middle of a Java Summit (a meeting at a coffee shop) one afternoon when he threw out this truism: When you share your pain, you cut it in half. Through our discussion, I added a corollary: When you share your joy, you double it.

When you share your pain, you cut it in half.
When you share your joy, you double it.

This is powerful when you think of the implications. Sharing your pain with someone cuts it in half because they feel with you. You're not alone in your pain. Our emotions must be seen and heard to be fully understood and processed; that's why sharing them is so powerful. Having someone there with you to literally or figuratively hold your hand can make a dramatic difference. Presence makes our journey easier to bear.

When we tell the truth about our hurt, others can help us heal.
—*Chip Dodd*

My grandfather had two mules named Nick and Jim. He would often say they were "the best two mules in Calloway County." He yoked them together to plow his fields. One mule couldn't pull the plow, but two could. It works with humans just like it works with mules: a load shared is a load easier carried.

My grandfather, with Nick and Jim, late 1940s

On the flip side, sharing your joy will double it. Most folks are happy when they hear good news; once you've shared, there are two of you and twice as much joy. There's another person who's as happy as you are.

Presence makes the journey of both pain and joy easier to bear.

Every time I repeat that truism and its corollary during a workshop, it resonates with someone. They know it's true because they've been there. They've experienced it themselves.

Most have no one to talk to

I was having another Java Summit at a different coffee shop with a friend. We'd met several times and gotten to know each other well. He was looking at his coffee as he thanked me for making the effort to be connected. Then he said, "I don't have anyone in my life that I share with like this. I haven't had this in a long time." His words hit me hard. I'd seen it in others, and I knew in my heart it was true for most, but I'd never heard it said so plainly.

The great heart-hunger of humanity is loneliness.
—William George Jordan

It really struck me. I've known many people in the same place. I experience this over and over when I talk to people. We've all got stuff inside us that needs to get out, but no one is there to listen to it.

A lesson from prison

I've been to prison twice . . . but not how you might be thinking. I'll get to that in a minute.

Most of my prison knowledge comes from movies, so maybe it doesn't really count. We've probably seen a few of the same movies. Most prison movies include a scene or a reference to a punishment they only use in prison: solitary confinement.

I hope you've seen the movie *The Shawshank Redemption*. If not, it's required viewing—put that on your list. At one point in the movie, Andy (Tim Robbins) gets put into solitary confinement for thirty days. It must have been pretty tough on him, because he came out of it looking like a train wreck.

Why is solitary confinement considered punishment? Because we're wired for connection. We need meaningful interaction with others. Prison wardens have already figured this out. It's interesting that the same punishment used against those in prison is the one we often impose on ourselves.

We know that we were made for connection, yet we don't seek it. It's the very definition of cognitive dissonance: believing and knowing one thing yet living another. It's a recipe for an unfulfilled life.

My first trip to prison was as a military aviator. Part of my training included being captured by the enemy as a prisoner of war (POW). A couple of times, I was confined to a small box for twenty minutes. *Confined* is a nice way to put it; it was more like jammed in—stuffed in, I would say. Thank goodness I'm not claustrophobic! I heard one guy have a breakdown when they tried to put him in the box.

I was put in solitary confinement several times in the prison camp. While in solitary, they encouraged us to communicate (surreptitiously, on the down low) with the other prisoners by using the tap code. It was developed by POWs during the Vietnam War and is like Morse code. Even the military knows we need each other. They know it so much that they created a way for people to stay connected, even in the most trying of times.

Code-switching

Code-switching occurs when we alter our persona, depending on the situation. It may mean shifting from formal to informal language, wearing different clothing, or changing hairstyles. For example, a person who code-switches might present one version of themselves at work but become someone else in the company of friends.

Consider tattoos as an example. Someone with tattoos on their arms might wear a short-sleeved shirt with friends; however, at work, they wear long sleeves to cover their tattoos.

Significant code-switching can be isolating: it implies that we're hiding who we truly are. Ideally, situations wouldn't require code-switching. Most people want to be fully known, but outlets for such honesty are scarce. Everyone code-switches to an extent, because fitting in is a powerful motivator; peer pressure is often the trigger for it.

When we listen in honest conversation, with no agenda except investing time in another person, we begin to see them as they are. Their code-switching diminishes, and they become more fully known. This is where connection happens.

Too Many Distractions

I have several friends who are airline pilots. Some fly short domestic trips; others travel overseas, sometimes on seventeen-hour flights with multiple pilots. You might take off, fly for several hours, rest, fly again, nap, then land on the other side of the world.

An airplane cockpit is a unique social laboratory. For hours, it's a captive environment. There's nowhere to go; your choices are silence, talking, or listening. You get to know people quickly because there's no one else and boredom sets in.

If you've taken a road trip, you've been in such a laboratory. It's just you and your passenger. I've taken my children to the store to create this environment, as it can stimulate conversation. Usually, there are too many distractions for meaningful conversation; we're simply too busy.

Back in the cockpit, it often feels like a confessional. People go through difficult things and need to share it with someone. If those feelings don't come out in a healthy way, they'll emerge elsewhere in unhealthy ways. In such scenarios, friendship forms rapidly. Combine this with the reality that most adults have few people who genuinely care about what they have to say.

As a military aviator, I've found myself in such a cockpit countless times. I have over 6,000 flight hours (that's about 260 days) in planes all over the world. One friend calls the C-130 the "four-fan trash can." Look at pictures of the C-130 and you'll understand why.

On one mission, I left Nashville in a C-130, headed west, and kept going. We flew around the world in seventeen days. Our stops included Hawaii, the Marshall Islands, Palau, Diego Garcia in the Indian Ocean, and the Azores in the Atlantic. When people say 70 percent of the earth is water, I believe them; I've seen a lot of it.

I've spent endless hours in cockpit laboratories. After a while, even the ocean and clouds lose their appeal. At such times, great conversation happens, because there are no distractions.

We know when it's fake

At a dinner, I sat next to a military man. I can usually spot military people in a crowd; it takes one to know one. It's easy if you know what to look for. He mentioned he was an aviator (I wasn't surprised) and asked if I was familiar with airplanes. I wondered if I was being punked and almost looked around for a camera.

"Yes, I know military airplanes," I responded. I didn't mention my military aviation career. He shared his background with a certain aircraft. I didn't reveal that I'd guessed his plane before he said it. Like I said, I know what to look for.

I showed him a photo of a plane he had flown—a picture I'd personally taken years ago, clearly not a stock image. He made a few factual comments, then changed topics.

Those were his only remarks. No questions. No "Where did you get that picture?" Or "Were you military?" Nothing. He talked almost exclusively about himself, offered only the bare minimum of courtesy, and gave no depth to the conversation. The façade was thin—a memorable conversation for the wrong reasons.

The takeaway: strive to be genuine, or don't try at all. It's so easy to see when someone is faking it. If you think you're fooling someone, you're not. You'll hear me repeat this often, because authenticity is so important to connection.

There are givers and takers

Once you sense that someone isn't truly listening, you lose interest in continuing. It feels pointless; you may as well be talking to yourself.

At another Java Summit, I spent time with a friend who is a remarkable conversationalist. He does many things well: asks open-ended questions, shows curiosity, and demonstrates excellent body language.

He made an insightful comment. "In life, there are givers and there are takers—and I'm done with takers." That observation offers a sound lesson. We quickly learn who gives and who takes. Givers put others first; takers focus on themselves.

Givers put others first in conversation; takers put themselves first.

Human nature prompts us to put ourselves first; this usually doesn't end well. In authentic conversation, strive to be a giver. This trait is rare and memorable.

Many takers aren't even aware of their behavior; I don't mean to disparage them, as most are truly oblivious.

Life is a Toby Keith song

People want to talk about themselves. Again, that's no surprise. They seek someone—anyone—who will listen. For most, life is a Toby Keith song: "I Wanna Talk about Me." That's the subject that interests them most. In all fairness, it's an excellent song: Keith captured human nature well.

A few years ago, I sold a mower. We arranged for a man to pick it up the next day. When he arrived, he briefly remarked on the beauty and quiet of our neighborhood. I had barely nodded before he launched into a long, detailed story about land he owned in a similar area embroiled in a lawsuit.

He spoke for several minutes. I tried making comments, but he didn't listen. He either missed my attempts or ignored them entirely. I thought, I expected you to buy a mower, not talk about yourself. He saw a situation vaguely familiar and used it to steer the conversation toward him.

You've seen this, too; it happens constantly. People routinely hijack conversations in person and on social media. People want to share their own stories—they just want someone who will listen.

> *Remember that the people you are talking to are a hundred times more interested in themselves and their wants and their problems than they are in you and your problems.*
> —Dale Carnegie

When you encounter someone intent on discussing only themselves, let them. Stay as long as you wish, but let them continue. Don't try to force the conversation into something it won't become; that only leads to frustration. Jump on their bandwagon if you like, ride as long as you want, and then move on when the ride is no longer a good one.

THE ART OF THE PAUSE IN OTHERS
During conversation, watch for the pause: the wrinkle in the brow, eyes cast aside or upward, a head tilt in thought, all mired in emotion. Wait for it. Don't fill the silence with words.

This waiting is counterintuitive to our instincts. Don't push your thoughts on them. Trust that they'll find words for their feelings. This window is vital for self-discovery.

Such moments are healthy. If you try to name their emotions, you might derail their process; at best, you guess correctly, but more likely you don't, and at worst, you disrupt their journey. Let them have their moment.

THE ART OF THE PAUSE IN YOURSELF
One person I know has alienated friends by ignoring the art of the pause: they'll give an eight-minute monologue all about themselves, with no breaks or opportunities for others to interject.

Have you talked to Mr. Stream-of-Consciousness, who rarely pauses for breath? It's exhausting and puzzling. I sometimes marvel at how they do it instead of engaging with the conversation.

It reminds me of survival school's simulated POW camp. During an interrogation, an officer swore at me for two minutes straight. About halfway through, I had an almost out-of-body experience just admiring his skill. This guy was good! He'd been cussing for a full minute without repeating a single word—and then went another minute with all new material. I was genuinely amazed. That day, I heard cuss words I didn't even know existed.

It also reminds me of a didgeridoo—an Aboriginal wind instrument played with circular breathing: inhaling through the nose while exhaling through the mouth. I've met people who can talk in this way. Being with them is emotionally draining.

The art of the pause allows others a chance to join in. Some people need more time to respond; the pause gives them room to maneuver. Without it, you block them out and just "carry on," as my mother would say—and that's not a compliment.

> *The right word may be effective, but no word was ever as effective as a rightly timed pause.*
> —Mark Twain

The pause also works after they speak. Silence lets them know you're considering their words. You can lead with, "Hmm. Let me digest that for a moment." It's a powerful phrase that adds suspense to the conversation.

Tempo influences conversation: slow down. Be intentional about your pace; slower is better than faster, which can be exhausting. Breathe and pause for effect.

Get used to pausing before speaking. Emotions can lead us to say things we regret. Give your smart brain time to catch up and present the best you.

More Toby Keith Fans

Some people merely need another breathing person nearby while they talk. They won't notice whether you're listening; those who do won't care and will continue regardless.

You've met parents who live vicariously through their children (also Toby Keith fans). They love telling you about their talented kids, playing Mozart at eight and taking college classes. That's great. Love that for you. A little bit of humble brag goes a long way.

The rest of us have smart children, good grades, and loving families... but there are few places to truly share those things. Grandparents are the safest outlet for that. Everywhere else is risky.

It's hard to tell someone they talk about themselves too much. It takes moral courage, or perhaps alcohol: in vino veritas. Most won't listen. Sometimes it's well received; sometimes not. Your mileage may vary.

How to connect

One of the best ways to connect with others is to be genuine. Get in the deep end of the pool, and share your challenges. Just be you. Ask deep questions, and listen.

Don't pretend your life is perfect. I know it's not; mine isn't either. We're all dealing with our own stuff.

Don't overshare—cringeworthy!—but if the opportunity arises, you can mention some challenges. For instance: "I'm familiar with family drama. Don't we all have more than we want! But go ahead; you were talking about your brother's marriage. Keep going." Don't hijack the conversation and make it about you. Briefly mention your experience, then turn the conversation back to the other person. In one workshop, a young fireman said, "When I'm talking to someone, I want to learn something I didn't know." His open-minded approach is authentic and attractive in conversation. It brings an inquiring mind into the scene.

Presence is a key ingredient

Our lives are far too busy. We're overwhelmed and underheard because our calendars are packed; that makes time and presence invaluable. You invest in another person. Time is precious, and it's impactful when you give it to someone else; you set aside yourself and your priorities to focus on them.

Presence is vital in conversation. We rush through so many moments, where half of us is here and the other half somewhere else. But the person in front of you deserves your full attention. Guard against the pull of your phone. Your digital life can wait. The life that matters is the one unfolding right here, right now.

Presence is the beginning of connection, and listening is the currency.

I sat with a dear friend through several chemo treatments. I always joked about it, telling him the main reason I came was for the free packs of crackers they gave out. As I reflect, I realize those times were the essence of presence. I regret not going more often; I wanted him to know I cared, with no agenda, just presence.

People want to know that *someone truly cares about them*. One way to show this is by being present: with their feelings, victories, and pain.

People say powerful things

I reconnected with an old colleague; he was always genuine. There was no façade. I found his authenticity attractive—what you see is what you get.

At a Java Summit, he said something profound. He looked me in the eye, and I knew the conversation was about to get real. He said, "I've been praying for genuine people to come into my life." I paused, letting the significance settle. It was a meaningful moment.

I've been praying for genuine people to come into my life.

We Long for Genuine Conversation

I wrote his words in my journal as we sat together; they were impactful for both of us and I didn't want to forget. I also wanted him to appreciate the significance of his statement. More on writing things down later.

We're wired for connection. We hunger for genuine relationships. We're made for someone to share life with, and it doesn't have to just be a spouse.

We need many people in our lives to complete us. We know it in our hearts. We can ignore it temporarily, but long-term neglect exacts a price. It's a thing of joy to find genuine people; we stay close to them because we desperately need that connection.

CHAPTER 3

The Mindshift

—⚋—

The great charm of conversation consists less in the display of one's own wit and intelligence than in the power to draw forth the resources of others.
—Jean de La Bruyère

I HAVE AN AIRLINE PILOT FRIEND who was paired with the same pilot for an extended period. Normally, they fly together for only a few days; this time, it was for about a month. After several days, he noticed every conversation was redirected to the other pilot and his land purchase in north Texas. My friend decided to test his intuition.

In the middle of a conversation, a few days later, he casually mentioned he had bought 160 acres in Wyoming—a fact he hadn't shared before. The other pilot immediately replied, "Did I mention that I bought forty acres in north Texas?" He repeated this experiment several times, and each time, the response was the same.

We're naturally self-centered; it's how we're wired. That's why it makes the news when a good Samaritan rescues someone from a burning car, risking their own safety. They put someone else ahead of themselves, and we marvel because we know it's not typical. It's exceptional.

I propose what I call a mindset shift, or "mindshift": be more like the good Samaritan. Put others before yourself.

LIFE IS BUSY.

Most of the time, we don't allow enough time; we're always overbooked. When my calendar is full, I struggle to listen and be present. I always feel there's something else to do or somewhere else to be.

We must give ourselves the mental space for conversation. This is one of many reasons not to be busy. Let's stop cramming our days and leave room for a conversation with no agenda. Give yourself permission to invest in someone else for a few minutes. Not every discussion leads to a solution or has an agenda—sometimes, just be present.

THE PROVING GROUNDS WITH MY DAD

How do we get there? The age-old question: Heredity or environment? Nature or nurture? For me, the answer was a little of both.

My mother was a great listener, so I inherited some of it. For the environmental part, my father contributed. My parents divorced when I was in first grade, and, like most children, I lived with my mother. As I grew, I began to understand a little of why she left.

When I became a teenager, I wanted a relationship with my father. I went along with anything just to be around him on Sunday afternoons. Most of these afternoons were spent at the kitchen table, while he smoked a pack of cigarettes and talked about how my mother shouldn't have left him. This was before concerns about secondhand smoke.

He would "give her down the road"—speak negatively about her. For me, I was on her side, but I never let on about my true feelings. I just patiently listened as he carried on about what happened. Again, I loved my father and would go along just to spend time with him.

Even as a teenager, I knew he had to get it out of his system. I wanted to help him get past the divorce, but he never did. There are a few formative experiences in a child's life, and those times with my father were certainly that. That experience taught me how to let things go in one ear and out the other. I could come home to my mother afterward and not dwell on the things he said about her.

This "letting go" is important when we're talking with people. We often struggle because of the emotional baggage we bring from the last conversation, or a similar situation we've faced with someone else. Practicing "catch and release" in conversation is important; you have to decide what to do with all that baggage.

I know you can't forget the past, just as I haven't forgotten those afternoons with my father. However, be as assertive as you can about not letting it burden you. I find that talking to yourself helps tremendously. Tell yourself where you want to be and remind yourself often. The more you say it out loud, the more it sinks in.

It's all about managing expectations

I used to work with a great guy named Marty; one of his mantras was "Let's manage expectations." If your objective is to have a great conversation, don't plan to talk about yourself much. This is your new expectation. This will be challenging, since we're wired to talk about ourselves.

Decide that you'll mentally and emotionally invest in the other person. Your goal during the conversation is to focus on their agenda. I know that's counterintuitive; however, remember your objective: a great conversation. Let them lead the dance. Yield your agenda to theirs. If you find yourself leading, give it back as soon as possible.

If you adopt the expectation that you won't be talking about yourself, you'll have a great conversation and be comfortable spending most of the time on the other person.

The closer you can get to matching expectations and reality, the more content you'll be.

Let's manage expectations. Not everyone will want to get in the deep end of the pool. Not everyone will ask questions about you, want to hear what you have to say, or offer the courtesy of listening. It may not be obvious or direct, but it will happen.

If I expect every conversation to get into the deep end of the pool, I'll be disappointed. Don't expect it often. I would say, expect the worst and be pleasantly surprised when something else shows up. Enjoy it when it does.

G**REAT CONVERSATIONALISTS ARE GOOD AT SELF-MANAGEMENT**

Great conversationalists are skilled at managing their thoughts and feelings. It's against our nature to put the other person first, but that's exactly what they do; they stay focused on the other person.

Self-management is a building block of emotional intelligence. Recognizing who we are and how we're wired is crucial to success.

Key concept: We are hard-wired to talk about ourselves.

Once you grasp that, use that knowledge to manage and adjust behavior. To have a great conversation, let's set aside our natural inclination to talk about ourselves.

Many years ago, as a second lieutenant living in Sacramento, I drove a 1968 Triumph Spitfire convertible. It was British racing green and a joy to drive with the top down in the California sun. If you've ever driven or ridden in a convertible, you understand the feeling.

Wanting to relive that experience, I bought another convertible a few years ago. Months after my purchase, I was telling a friend about my new car. They immediately redirected the conversation, telling a story about their own recent car purchase. It wasn't malicious, but it further confirmed the strong inclination to talk about ourselves.

When I tell a story like that, I want my friend to celebrate with me—not turn the conversation to them. The last thing I want to hear is, "Yeah, I got a new car too. A few months ago, my friend sold me a car just like I wanted, and I got a great deal." Many people do that. I don't think it's intentional; they simply don't consider the timing.

Great conversation is about the other person, not you. Perhaps you did get a great deal on your car months ago . . . but now isn't the time to share it. Celebrate with your friend today; you can tell your story another time.

Every journey begins with the first step

Great conversation is about the other. When we're all in, we set ourselves aside and listen like Nate. It's their agenda; they lead the dance. Some people struggle with that. Again, putting the other person first is counterintuitive—a fundamental mindshift, but essential.

Put the other person first.

If you can put the other person before you, the rest of this book will come naturally for you. You may be thinking, That's a tough one; I'm not sure I can do it.

I understand. It's tough. Life is a Toby Keith song—I want to talk about me.

Start with small steps. Try it for a few minutes when the stakes are low, perhaps with a five-year-old. If you mess up, it's fine. It may feel counterintuitive, but you'll improve with practice.

Act your way into feelings . . .

Don't wait until you feel like doing it. If you wait for that, the feeling may never come. None of us start an exercise program because we feel like going to the gym. The feeling will come, but not on the first day.

Begin by acting your way into feelings. Tell yourself you'll put the other person first. Seriously: talk to yourself. Affirm that you're interested in the other person and do want to know more. Say it aloud. Hearing it helps you internalize the message. Yes, it's a mind game—but it works. I've seen it work.

. . . BECAUSE FEELINGS FOLLOW ACTION

When we act out the feelings we desire, our feelings follow.

Feelings follow action—it doesn't work the other way around. Keep doing the right thing, and the feeling will come.

I joined the US Air Force because I thought it was what I was supposed to do. When I first joined, it wasn't because I was especially patriotic. I didn't understand that I was defending freedom and serving something bigger than me. After I'd been in for a while, those feelings came—and they came on strong.

We've all made New Year's resolutions to go to the gym. It's a great goal, and we go often at first. But by mid-February, there's no wait at the treadmills. Most people who made those resolutions are gone. What happened?

One of our challenges as humans is that we prefer the easy life. Pain, effort, and struggle take a back seat to rest and relaxation. We don't feel like going to the gym. It's hard.

Remember: Don't wait until you feel like going. Those who stopped going to the gym hoped the feeling would arrive, but it doesn't work that quickly. You need to act first. Go to the gym even when you don't feel like it. After several trips, the desire begins to develop. The feelings come after the action. You act your way into those feelings.

Now, apply this concept to your conversations. It's counterintuitive to put others ahead of you, to speak less and not interrupt. Begin by practicing those behaviors, with a sincere desire to develop those feelings. Begin by doing some of the things you've read about.

Again, I recommend speaking your desired feelings aloud. It's as simple as saying, "I want to be a person who speaks less and doesn't interrupt others." When you combine intentional actions with affirming the feelings you want to develop, those feelings follow.

Start from a Place of No Judgment

Imagine you and I are having a conversation about some issues you're facing. It goes without saying, but I'll say it: I have troubles too.

Imagine we each put our troubles in a cardboard box, then walk into a room with a big round table. There are ten other people, all carrying boxes of different sizes. None of the boxes are tiny.

The facilitator instructs us to place our boxes on the table and stand beside them. We shuffle over, place our boxes, and look around the room. Some make eye contact; others don't. The facilitator says, "Open the flaps on your box. Walk around the table and look inside these boxes."

Some boxes you'll cautiously peer into and say, "I don't want any part of that one," or "That looks really tough." By the time you finish, most of us are glad to pick up our own box and leave.

Here's the point: We're all carrying a box of troubles; none of us get a pass. We've all got junk. We're all broken in different ways, and most of us try to hide it. It doesn't matter how great our lives appear or how much success we have in the eyes of man, none of us have it all together.

We're all carrying a box of troubles.
We're all broken humans.

Keep that mental image in mind when you're talking to someone: we all have a box of troubles. Your troubles may have a different name, but they're still troubles. This keeps us aware that we're all broken humans—with frailties, challenges, and insecurities. Remembering that helps us stay humble and avoid judgment. Looking down from the moral high ground won't help your conversation.

When I described this to a friend, he agreed wholeheartedly. His words were powerful and emotional: "I'm one of you—wounded and flawed. I've got junk too. Different name, but it's still junk. I'm an emotional cripple." I thought, Aren't we all? If we remember that, we keep ourselves grounded.

Listen without judgment. Keep an open mind. Always remember you're just as broken as they are. Keeping this in mind keeps you grounded. Your issues may be different, but just as complex.

All this may sound sentimental, and maybe it is, but it's true and it works. These approaches put us on equal footing with others. They inspire humility, which is essential to meaningful conversation.

REMEMBER YOUR OBJECTIVE

We live in a busy world. Modern society worships at the altar of effectiveness and efficiency, always measuring output and seeking ways to do more. Let's remember why we're here. Shift your mindset to focus on your objective: Are you pursuing a decision or sale, or a meaningful conversation?

A great conversation is counterintuitive to efficiency. It may not seem productive, but have the courage to define success in your own terms, not someone else's. Don't let the universe define it for you. In this case, conversation minus agenda equals success.

Conversation - Agenda = Success

Some will say they don't have time for a conversation without an agenda, with no tangible output at the end; I encourage you to consider it from another angle.

Think about it: all the great and meaningful things in life can't be held in your hand. Love, family, connection, and friendship immediately come to mind; you can't buy these things or grasp them, but they create moments we remember for a long time. These intangibles are what make life wonderful.

In conversations with this as our goal, the relationship is the result—the outcome we seek. Don't tie every discussion to efficiency or task completion; sometimes, moving the ball down the field in a relationship is done simply by being present and listening. Maintaining presence with another person is a rare and magical thing. Remember Nate? I'm still talking about him; he's simply that rare and memorable.

When you enter a discussion, identify your objective. Do you want to land a point? Are you willing to risk a friendship to do that? Or do you want to increase the connection with this person? Identifying your goal can help you decide how you'll conduct yourself during your time together. It's like choosing a hat to wear; remember, you can only wear one at a time. If you're wearing the "make the connection" hat or the "have a great conversation" hat, you'll approach your time differently than if you're wearing the "I need to pass along information" or "I need to tell this person what to do" hat.

Our objective is to have a great conversation. Defining success helps us identify tactics that will help us reach it. Remind yourself of your objective before you begin the conversation.

Be genuinely interested in the other person

Develop a genuine interest in the other person; let them see that you care. I don't like the phrase "Fake it till you make it"; it implies there's no real feeling for the other person, and it doesn't capture the essence of what we're after. That might work once or twice, but people will quickly see through it.

Sometimes we struggle to move to a new place of thinking; we want to be there, but it's hard. First, we tell ourselves where we want to be; after that, we tell others. With these two things, your own words will come true before your eyes. Being accountable to yourself and others will help you on the road of becoming that person.

Telling others triggered this book. I've wanted to write a book for many years, but I didn't get serious about it until I told someone that I was writing a book. Once you do that, you're committed. You have thrown it out there; now you have to live up to it. It's an effective technique, trust me. It becomes the self-fulfilling prophecy: when you speak it again and again, it will come true.

Another way to cultivate a genuine interest in others is to always believe you can learn something from everyone; this will keep you from putting yourself on a pedestal. It brings a collegiate, co-learning tone to your discussions. No one wants to be around someone who thinks they're better than everyone else.

Always look for the learning moment. Curiosity is such a powerful and attractive place to dwell, because the world comes to you in interesting ways. People will say the most compelling things if you're listening for them.

On the other hand, we can sense when there's no curiosity. We can see when someone has made up their mind on a topic. When I sense this, I say as little as possible; then I change the subject as soon as I can.

DON'T CORRECT THEM WHEN THE STAKES ARE LOW

Recently, a friend was telling me about the latest iPhone update and its features. I'd researched the latest release and was familiar with it. My friend stated something as fact that I knew was not true, but I chose to let it go. It was an insignificant point that disappeared within five seconds of being said. What good would it have done to correct them when the stakes were so low?

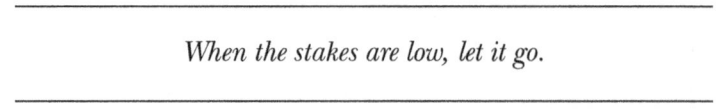

When the stakes are low, let it go.

Let go of always being right. Don't waste your energy in a disagreement about unimportant points. Save the hard discussions for when it matters, and try to live in a place where you don't always have to be right. A little humility goes a long way; without it, you'll struggle to connect. Even when you know you're right, weigh the cost of correcting someone.

- Is it worth it?
- Will correcting them make any real difference in the conversation?

It doesn't help to correct every little thing, but some people enjoy the feeling of superiority that comes with it. Always needing to be right often points to a shortfall in emotional intelligence. After a while, being around that person isn't enjoyable. A little bit of that goes a long way.

Choose your battles. If it's worth it, speak out; if not, let it go. Have the maturity and mental flexibility to let someone else take the upper hand. Don't allow yourself to be drawn into a meaningless disagreement.

Being gracious in your conversation is another way to let go. Before I retired from the US Air Force, I was in a grocery store—not in uniform—and I bumped into someone who worked at my Wing while I was the Wing Commander. I was two or three levels above this person on the organizational chart.

We were sharing small talk when he asked, "Are you still out there?" Meaning, are you still serving as a military member at the Wing where I am? I smiled and said, "Yeah, I'm still out there." Inside, I was laughing, but I maintained a poker face.

As a military aviator, we had a phrase for that: catastrophic loss of situational awareness. Not recognizing the senior executive of the company you're working for, to his face, would certainly qualify! But what good would it have done to belittle or berate him by saying, "Yes, I'm your boss's boss, and you should know who I am." A little grace in our conversation goes a long way; besides, it's good for the soul to be able to laugh at yourself. Grace and kindness are gifts that cost you nothing.

Don't tell everything when it doesn't matter

I was working with a client on a product delivery issue. There was a mix-up, but it all worked out and the client was satisfied. Afterward, it became clear the client had made an assumption that was not true. As they were describing it, I felt they weren't capturing the essence of what was going on.

Here's the thing: in this situation, it didn't matter. As long as the client doesn't think I dropped the ball or failed to deliver, I'm content. I kept my thoughts to myself; it would have taken too much effort to straighten it out and may have harmed the relationship. The juice wasn't worth the squeeze.

There are times when you don't need to share everything in your head. Consider the stakes. If this is the hill you must die on, then stand firm; but you don't get to choose many hills like that. We have to let some things slide. Have grace in your conversations, and choose your battles carefully.

Don't have an agenda

Set your agenda aside when you begin the conversation. Your goal is to let them lead. Agendas lead to closed-off thinking and overcontrolling, traits counterproductive to a good conversation. You must leave room for their thoughts.

A friend once told me, "You're the first person who has not had an agenda when they talk to me; you're not trying to fix me." I don't listen to fix people; it's not my place. Besides, I'm not sure I know how to fix anybody. Still, I felt a tug at my heart. This person found someone with whom they could be their real self. In that moment, I knew I was able to let them be fully seen.

When we speak of someone having an agenda, we omit the word that should accompany it: hidden. It's an agenda they don't wish to disclose. That hidden agenda tends to guide responses. My suggestion? Leave hidden agendas at home. Better yet, leave all agendas behind. If you must have an agenda, state it up front. Get it out there and don't try to hide it.

The agenda-less conversation fills a needed space inside us. I met someone for a Java Summit a while back. It was our second or third time getting together, and we talked for about an hour about whatever topic came up. Later, I received a text from him: "It's a good thing for me to have these meetings with no agenda, pretense, or necessary goal. Thank you, my friend." I didn't want anything from him, and I didn't have a hidden agenda; I simply wanted to stay connected because he was a great guy.

Another friend made a powerful statement echoing the same feeling: "I long for conversation with open-minded people." In other words, someone willing to listen without being driven by an agenda. Be ready to walk with someone on their journey and let them decide where it goes. It's worthwhile.

Life can be an adventure when you let someone else drive.

I met Vince in Phoenix. He was my rideshare driver as I traveled from the airport to the hotel. Vince and I dove into the deep end of the pool pretty quickly. He intentionally took longer fares, giving him the opportunity to converse with someone.

He turned out to be quite skilled at it, so I asked how he learned. He said, "I was a server in Las Vegas for eighteen years. My whole career and pay system were based on making the connection." We talked about asking questions to dig deeper, and he said something key: "I ask my riders about things I would care about if I were in their seat." That's the example of pursuing someone else's agenda. I may never meet Vince again, but I'll remember him because he knows how to have a good conversation.

Part of not having an agenda is being patient; you have to go at their speed and can't get ahead of them. If they want to stop at a rest stop, stay with them. If they pause to admire something, stand there and patiently admire it as well. Move at their speed and set your agenda aside as you pursue theirs. In that time, remain true to yourself. Don't be a chameleon, but remember: *Sempre Gumby* (always flexible).

SPEAK LESS THAN THE OTHER PERSON

We've already established that people like to talk about themselves. This isn't a bad thing; it's just how we're wired. Let's acknowledge this and move to the next step: enable the other person to talk more than you.

A great conversation keeps the other person talking.

This can backfire if you take it to the extreme, since it can seem like you're disinterested if you don't say much. Look for the sweet spot. I convey my engagement through nonverbal cues, sometimes jumping in, saying something, then jumping out, just to let them know I'm beside them on the journey. I approach this through genuine curiosity. People say the most interesting things, but I can't hear them if I'm talking.

Focus on self-awareness

We're wired to think highly of ourselves; our opinions are obviously the best ones to have—that's why we've chosen them. It's not strange to think like this; we all have these thoughts and are naturally vested in ourselves.

If we're not careful, this self-interest can show up in our conversations. Our natural inclination is to talk about ourselves, but some people don't have the self-awareness to notice how much they do it. Others can be self-absorbed and unconcerned about your thoughts. They know they talk about themselves a lot, and it doesn't bother them. I've met a few of these, but the majority are simply not self-aware.

Remember that the conversation is about them, not you. Put them first; set yourself aside and focus on the other person. Yes, we're wired to think of ourselves first, but I suggest aggressively putting this feeling aside for a few moments to have a great conversation.

When I encounter someone who talks a lot about themselves, part of me is tempted to quote a line from *The Shawshank Redemption*: "How can you be so obtuse?" It didn't go well when Andy Dufresne said this to the warden. Someone who is obtuse doesn't catch on quickly; they're slow on the draw. Andy ended up in solitary confinement—ouch. It would likely have the same effect on the person you're speaking with, so I can't recommend it.

If you have never asked yourself, "Do I talk about myself too much?"— the answer might be yes. Here is the magic, though: asking yourself this question will make you more aware of it during your conversations and help you focus on the other person.

Remember the 80/20 rule

My goal in every conversation is to listen 80 percent of the time and speak 20 percent. I don't literally track a word count, but I try to be aware of it. It's not hard, because most people want to talk about what's on *their* mind. Remember, it's a Toby Keith song.

Listen more, speak less.

Listen more than you talk. You've heard the saying that God gave you two ears and one mouth for a reason—He knew what He was doing. Epictetus, a Greek philosopher, echoed this sentiment when he said, "We have two ears and one mouth so we can listen twice as much as we speak."

Set yourself aside. Think of listening as a practice when you enter a conversation. Throw a question out, then sit back and listen with no agenda. When you learn to listen well, you move into a category with little competition.

The deadliest character trait is pride; the greatest virtue is humility

Setting yourself aside requires humility. Compare pride with humility, and ask yourself which is more attractive. If you're not sure, ask yourself this: Would you rather take a road trip with pride or humility? Many positive things flow from humility; the opposite is true of pride. Pride talks about itself and how great its life is, but never considers that your life could be great as well and certainly never asks about it.

We see this on social media. There's a place for sharing your life with those around you, but much of it tends toward how great life is. After a while, you can only take so much, and you have to mute or unfollow. Pride is well represented in the phrase "A little bit goes a long way." If you find yourself talking a lot about your own life and situation, stop right where you are. Cut off midsentence with, "All right, enough about my life. Tell me about your family." Give someone else a chance to share how great their life is, and listen to them when they do.

I listened to a podcast recently—the guest was an expert in a field I wanted to investigate. However, the host talked more than the guest, focusing on himself. He stacked questions (asking two or three in a row without waiting for the answer) and pontificated. A few times, he interrupted or cut off the guest while speaking. These are unattractive conversational qualities. The reason to have somebody on a podcast (and the reason I listen) is so the audience can hear from the guest, not the host. The host knew much about the subject, but the host was not the expert—the guest was. People, even podcast hosts, enjoy talking about themselves.

It is the province of knowledge to speak, and it is the privilege of wisdom to listen.
—*Oliver Wendell Holmes*

Think of conversation as a tennis match. I want the ball in their court 80 percent of the time. I want it on their side of the net for most of the conversation. This drives me toward open-ended questions that dig deeper into the why or how of what they just said. Keep the story on them by asking about their experiences. Don't rush to move the conversation forward until they're ready. Go on the journey with them.

Don't interrupt

Everyone has a good or funny story that relates to nearly any topic. You might want to interject, but when you keep the ball on the other side of the net, you probably won't get to say it. The art is to stay focused on the other person when your own story comes to mind. They decide where you're going. Let them lead the dance. Your great story may have to wait for another conversation.

When I'm in conversation, I keep something nearby to write on. I take many notes when talking with people. Sometimes, interrupting thoughts arise, such as a story or something for my to-do list. If I don't release these thoughts, they dominate my attention. You think of it constantly because you don't want to forget it; it keeps you from being fully engaged in the present conversation.

When these interrupting thoughts or stories arise, I jot down a word or two to clear them from my mind so I can move on. This keeps me focused on the other person and their message. I might return to those thoughts, but I can't be too attached to them. If it's important, you'll have another chance.

At a workshop, a participant described the same struggle: a thought popped up and occupied his mind. His solution was to email himself quickly, freeing his attention for the moment.

The same advice applies when talking over someone: don't do it. Sometimes you must speak over someone, but be intentional. Don't make a habit of it; save it for when it's really necessary.

I was talking with a friend the other day, and he asked my opinion. "Do you think I should go with option A, or option B, or option C?" I made the mistake of interrupting with an answer (option A). They kept talking as if they hadn't heard me. A few minutes later, I made the mistake of doing it again, and they did the same thing. They finished their sentence as if they had never heard me, even though I'm certain they did. I relearned a lesson: Don't interrupt people. Wait for the pauses.

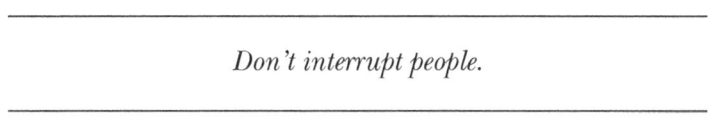

Don't interrupt people.

Interrupting short-circuits a person's communication process. It's a move that puts space between you and them.

Once I asked someone what bothers them most during communication: "I get frustrated by someone who thinks they know what I'm going to say. They interrupt and try to fill in with their own words." Neither is helpful. I understand that sometimes you feel compelled to interrupt. If you do, return the conversation quickly. Tell your story, but keep it brief. Give them the stage again. After you've spoken, say, "You know what, I interrupted you. Keep going. You were telling me about your friend's drinking problem."

Sometimes a person might struggle to think of the right word to say. As we're watching them think, we want to help, so we fill in the word we think they're trying to come up with. One day I asked a workshop participant what she thought about that: Does that work? Her answer was an emphatic and emotionally frustrated *no*. The whole room dogpiled in and agreed with her. Problem is, we all do it. We're trying to be helpful, we're trying to get there faster, but it's not helpful. It's detrimental to connection and communication.

Get comfortable with silence

> Fact One: We are terrible with silence.
> Fact Two: We want to fill the space.

This is why leaders ask their team a question, wait three seconds, and then answer it themselves. When it gets quiet, it seems strange. You ask a question and get silence; it can feel awkward.

The strangeness of silence is in its rarity. We live in a world of constant noise. When we're in the car, we listen to the radio or a podcast. At work, we listen to music to fill the space. At home, we can play background noise. White noise generators drive away silence. Silence is rare in our modern world.

The strangeness of silence is in its rarity.

Some say silence is awkward, especially in conversation. However, once you understand the power of silence, you'll want to embrace it.

Silence is a gift

In a great conversation, there comes a time when the struggle shows on their face. They look up, their eyes move side to side, or their brow wrinkles as they think deeply. They're struggling to find the right words for their feelings. When I see that struggle, silence right then is a gift. Don't interrupt their thoughts to fill the space. That's the time to be quiet and give them room to maneuver.

As an aviator, we would sometimes ask air traffic control (ATC) for permission to execute a nonstandard flight procedure. We would ask for "room to maneuver." In other words, "We'll be doing something nonstandard, so clear out the space for us." Just like ATC giving us airspace, silence gives the other person room to maneuver.

Don't fill in words for them or guess to finish their sentence. Be patient. The struggle and journey to find the right word is valuable. Give space for that journey, and wait patiently. Don't act hurried. You're trying to help by suggesting words, but it short-circuits the process. They may use your word, but it's not theirs, and your words don't mean as much to them as their own.

You'll know when it's time to speak again. Sometimes, after they finally respond, I say, "I knew you were on a journey, and I stayed quiet to let you go." It shows I respect their journey and am present with them.

Silence provides time and space for them to explore their thoughts. This is nonstandard because most people are waiting for their turn to talk. They don't see the space as sacred, so they jump in and trample whatever magic is happening with the other person.

This gift of silence is also powerful after they've said something meaningful. When someone shares something profound, your silence shows respect for their thoughts. A quiet pause gives them room to explore. Sometimes, a response is nothing more than "That's good." That allows them to linger a little longer. It also shows "I'm right there with you."

Silence is a lever that can move the world.

According to my friend Luis, silence is the game-changing superpower. I'd say he's right on the money. Ask a question, then wait quietly. Some people need time to process. If they don't want to answer, move on; your silence gives them space to decide. Resist the urge to fill the silence. Let it do its thing. Much goodness happens in the quiet.

Don't think about your response while they're still talking

I asked several people what traits great conversationalists possess. Many answered, "They're not thinking about what to say while I'm still talking."

Listening declines dramatically when we're busy planning our response. Multitasking doesn't work with tasks or people; something has to give. Our goal is to be fully present and to listen. Listen to understand, not to respond. I know that's counterintuitive.

Listen to understand, not to respond. Listening isn't waiting to talk.

Try not to think about what you'll say when they stop talking. Have you ever been in church when people start putting their things away during the closing prayer? They aren't listening anymore. The same thing happens when you begin thinking about your response before the other person finishes.

Tell yourself, "I'll listen fully before I formulate an answer." Remind yourself to avoid distractions. The more you practice, the better you'll get. Since this isn't the norm, use verbal techniques and body language to hold the space while you consider your answer. Examples include:

- You have a "thinking" look during your pause.
- "So . . . what I hear is . . ."
- "Let me think about that for a second."

These techniques can hold the space for your response and indicate that you're thinking. For group conversations, this may not work as well; group dynamics are different, and pauses are less effective.

BE MINDFUL OF YOUR BIASES AS THEY ARISE
We all have biases—mental shortcuts that help us solve challenges. Our brains are lazy and seek patterns, which become biases. I tend to turn right on red, since it's legal in most places and saves time.

Confirmation bias is familiar: we seek evidence that confirms our beliefs and ignore contradictory evidence. Politics illustrates this well. Conservative voters look at conservative news sources, and liberal voters at liberal sources. We discount news that doesn't support our bias and give more credit to news that does. We tend to live in echo chambers.

Biases aren't always bad. A friend is an emergency room doctor; in the ER, they use biases to diagnose quickly. Biases help us reach solutions faster.

However, we must be careful with our biases. If my bias is to turn right on red, but there's a sign reading "No turn on red," my bias won't help me. I can't always assume my bias is correct or useful.

In conversation, when an automatic thought surfaces, look for a bias. Once you recognize bias, you can begin to understand and control it.

If a conservative and a liberal are in conversation, they should both recognize their biases are pulling in opposite directions. This awareness helps control responses.

OUR BIASES LEAD TO ASSUMPTIONS
This is a tough one. We fill in gaps in our knowledge with assumptions. Challenge those assumptions before you get too far down the road with them.

One workshop participant addressed this directly. He was a young Black man with an extraordinary origin story. He said, "I grew up in a home with a white Jewish mother and a Black Nigerian father who was not Jewish. What's normal for me isn't normal for most. What's outside the box for you is inside the box for me."

Solutions that are "outside the box" to you are "inside the box" to someone else.

I appreciated his candor and immediately sensed a connection (remember the Johari window?). Transparency draws people in, much like moths to a flame. What he described wouldn't be apparent from his appearance, and making assumptions would miss those details. The more we know about others, the deeper our connection.

One colleague was married to a woman who had spent much of her childhood in Mexico City, where she learned Spanish. As an adult, she would use her Spanish when ordering at Mexican restaurants. What surprised the staff was that this White woman spoke Spanish with a Mexico City accent. Most people who look like her don't speak Spanish as fluently, and certainly not with that accent. The waitstaff made assumptions that were visibly challenged. Unchecked assumptions can hinder meaningful conversations.

If you discover you have made an incorrect assumption, recover promptly. You might even address it directly: for example, "You speak Spanish with a Mexico City accent. Tell me your story."

Another example is seeing someone wear a mask. Early in the COVID pandemic, everyone wore masks; in the years since, I've heard people make light of those who continue wearing them. Some view it as an overreaction. Yet the individual could be immunocompromised or ill and trying not to spread illness. We often fill in gaps and pass judgment on people without knowing their circumstances. Do your best to avoid this.

REMAIN FLEXIBLE IN YOUR THOUGHTS, AND WITHHOLD YOUR OPINIONS

Always assume there are aspects of a topic that you do not know. Even if you're Albert Einstein discussing nuclear physics and relativity, keep an open mind. Have the humility to believe that you always have something to learn. Your beliefs about a subject could be mistaken. At the very least, another person may offer a new perspective. Remain open-minded, at least temporarily, to alternate viewpoints.

That flexibility—and humility regarding your own opinions—fuels curiosity, leading to richer, more substantive conversations.

Don't cross the Bridge of Decision

Our judgments can divide us and create barriers to connection. They also erect walls that restrict meaningful conversation. Politics is a ready example of this. If I judge someone as being on the other side of the political spectrum, it can create in me an angst that's difficult to overcome. I've crossed the Bridge of Decision once that judgment is made. The mental journey to the other side of the river is complete. Problem is, that journey across the bridge is hard to backtrack. This limits the open-mindedness essential to good conversation.

These days, we're quick to label others. A hastily applied label can shape all subsequent thoughts about someone. They may be a wonderful person, yet a negative label can prevent us from discovering that.

Be curious, not judgmental.
—*Ted Lasso*

Suspending judgment means choosing not to cross the Bridge of Decision. When we suspend judgment, we admit that we lack sufficient information to make a definitive choice. The deeper our convictions, the more challenging it is to suspend judgment. It's easy to do so when discussing the merits of growing a beard; it's far more difficult with deeply felt issues like religion or politics. These things are close to the bone, as they say; they touch us personally. We must be vigilant with our emotions; unchecked, they may lead us to say things that hinder discussions or harm relationships.

Typically, judging another makes us feel superior, however subtle the feeling may be. That sense will be communicated, regardless of our efforts to suppress it. We must not take the moral high ground; others will perceive it, and it's ineffective. Years ago, while watching *Downton Abbey*, Violet Crawley, the Dowager Countess of Grantham, delivered a memorable line: "Does it ever get cold on the moral high ground?" Remind yourself that you're no better than anyone else; we all have faults, even if by different names. Walk alongside others, not above them.

Several years ago, I met an acquaintance at a coffee shop. Our conversation lasted perhaps ten minutes, but it stayed with me for days, for all the wrong reasons. I couldn't initially understand why, but the reason eventually became clear.

I'd recently accepted a promotion and was enthusiastically telling him about my new role. His response was, "Yes, a few years ago, I turned down that position." His tone and commentary felt belittling, as though saying, "I was offered the position you're excited about, but declined because I was too good for it." It cast a wet blanket on my enthusiasm.

I left with the impression that he felt superior. He may not have intended it, but I sure received it that way. Not only did he make it about himself, but he also minimized my achievement. I'd shared my excitement, only to have it dismissed. Next time he calls, I suspect I'll be busy with work. You know what I mean. I'm simply not interested.

LET'S TALK ABOUT EMOTIONS

No one would intentionally choose to win the battle but lose the war, yet that's what happens when we let emotions dictate our responses. Even when we're in the right, a harsh exchange may irreparably harm a relationship.

Is it worth it? Perhaps, depending on how important the topic is to you. If it is, stand your ground and go in with guns a'blazin. (As Wyatt Earp would say, "Skin that smokewagon and see what happens!") If not, maybe let it go. The rational person would let it go, but that person wasn't there two minutes ago when you yanked your emotional guns out of their holsters. Our emotions can lead us to say things we regret. That's when a pause or silence is especially useful—but you already knew that.

The inability to suspend judgment impedes fruitful conversations. Flexibility is vital; openness to other possibilities prevents judgmental attitudes. These are subtle signals, yet people are perceptive and notice them.

Sometimes, our preconceived ideas keep us from suspending judgment. Prejudices, assumptions, and biases place us in the Seat of Judgment. Avoid presuming you know the facts; suspending judgment allows an open mind.

I'm reminded of the time I saw a colleague at a restaurant. We worked together occasionally, but not closely. I didn't know her relationship status, and she was with a man who appeared to be much older. Ignoring the warning in my own mind, I asked, "Is that your dad?" She punched my shoulder and replied, "No! That's my husband!" Ouch. Open mouth, insert foot. Lesson learned: avoid assumptions. Next time I'll say, "Tell me about your friend."

Allow for alternate perspectives. You don't need to agree, but avoid rushing to judgment. Listen before forming your opinion. Crossing the Bridge of Decision shapes our thoughts, choices, and actions. Suspend judgment whenever possible. Keep an open mind.

You must also suspend judgment when you think you know where the conversation is headed. The phrase "wait for it" applies: see where the other person leads the discussion. Remember, it's a dance: let them lead.

> We do not need to judge nearly so much as we think we do. This is the age of snap judgments. The habit is greatly intensified by the sensational press. Twenty-four hours after a great murder there is difficulty in getting enough men who have not already formulated a judgment to try the case. These men, in most instances, have read and accepted the garbled, highly colored newspaper account; they have, to their own satisfaction, discovered the murderer, practically tried him, and sentenced him. We hear readers state their decisions with all the force and absoluteness of one who has had the whole Book of Life made luminant and spread out

before him. If there be one place in life where the attitude of the agnostic is beautiful, it is in this matter of judging others. It is the courage to say, "I don't know. I am waiting further evidence. I must hear both sides of the question. Till then I suspend all judgment." It is this suspended judgment that is the supreme form of charity.[7]

I love the phrase "the attitude of the agnostic." It's remarkable how much it conveys in so few words. The amazing thing is, that paragraph was written over a hundred years ago. People don't change.

The people you talk with aren't going to think the same way you do; they'll have different beliefs and opinions. They may disagree with your core beliefs about many things. Your ability to suspend judgment in these moments will help you have a substantive conversation. When someone's position is the opposite of yours, you must be able to grasp two opposing ideas and live with them for a while.

Suppose your friend believes the moon landing was a hoax. They're intelligent and appear rational; that should give you pause. You shouldn't think this person is foolish because they believe something different than you do. That would be crossing the Bridge of Decision.

If your best friend doesn't believe in the moon landing, will you be able to remain friends? A more difficult question would be, if you voted for one party and your friend voted for another, can you still be friends?

Our biases can have a significant impact on us. If someone is wearing a political party hat or has a party bumper sticker on their car, we can make assumptions and judgments about them that will affect our interactions. My advice: hold your biases captive. Don't let them lead you; you must lead them. Decide if they're true and whether they apply to the situation.

Don't let your biases lead you; you must lead them.

---

[7] William George Jordan, *The Kingship of Self Control.*

The Mindshift

As a military man, this concept resonates with me. When a distinguished visitor arrives at a military base, the senior ranking officer is among the first to greet them, shake their hand, and welcome them. As Wing Commander, I shook hands with many federal, state, and local officials; I also saluted several US presidents and vice presidents when they visited. They would land in Air Force One or Air Force Two, and I would wait at the bottom of the stairs to render a sharp salute as proper military courtesy. No matter their political party, no matter whom I voted for, I gave each one my best salute, shook their hand, and welcomed them warmly. I was intentional about not letting my political bias interfere with my official duties.

When we let our biases take over—when we pass judgment—our conversations can't be as fruitful as they might have been. Suspended judgment is the definition of tolerance. Your conspiracy theories about the moon landing may differ from mine, but I'll listen as though they weren't foreign to me. I also understand that you can think differently than I do, and that's fine. Tolerance doesn't mean affirmation; it simply means I'll listen and consider with an open mind, even if I don't initially agree with you.

I was in a meeting when a teammate gave a recap of his time helping those affected by a natural disaster. His observations about volunteers and people in need offered an interesting societal commentary. First, volunteers don't care about the political beliefs of those needing help; they simply want to help people. Second, people in need don't care about the political beliefs of the volunteers; they're grateful to be helped.

He then remarked that two things can be true at the same time. That's a powerful statement as we move forward in our efforts to engage with others.

In this case, two political beliefs can coexist in the same space and time. You believe what you wish, and I'll do the same. Even if our beliefs are polar opposites, let's not allow that to undermine our relationship.

Many years ago in high school, I was having a conversation with Mike, a Black friend on the football team with me. I have no idea how we arrived at this conversational crossroad, but we were talking about Santa

Claus at football practice. Yes, the strange things that high school boys talk about. At one point, I must have said something about Santa being White. Mike looked at me, eyebrows raised, and said, "No he's not, he's Black." I said, "He's not Black, he's White." He came right back with, "No he's not, Santa is Black!"

I remember that conversation as if it were yesterday. My friend opened my mind to possibilities I hadn't even considered. Yes: Santa can be both Black and White. That memory helps me mentally hold the idea of two opposing things being true at the same time.

Others will see the world differently than you. How do we truly connect in a polarized society that is becoming less and less tolerant? I'm not saying you must agree and affirm others, but you need to understand that they have different ideas and come from different places.

> Embracing the concept of dual truths can lead to greater emotional flexibility, improved problem-solving skills, enhanced ability to navigate complex situations, and increased empathy and understanding of others' perspectives. By recognizing that life is not always a matter of either/or, but often both/and, we can develop a more balanced and nuanced approach to our experiences and relationships.[8]

Suspending judgment takes mental agility and intentionality, but it places you in a favorable position for a meaningful conversation.

Keep your advice to yourself

You've been in conversations where someone wants to discuss their options for an impending decision. Sometimes they'll ask for advice and truly mean it. Other times, they might ask but not actually want to hear it. They just want to talk.

I try to stick to the troubleshooting approach, discussing options and weighing pros and cons. After that, I step back to let them decide. I want

---

[8] Meg Davis.

them to own the decision, so I rarely say what I would do. I outline possibilities, then give them space to choose their course of action. At times, I may point out another reality or a different way to look at the situation, but only when they're receptive. Such moments are like an open door. I'll walk through, but I rarely push my way in.

I also consider the permanence of the decision. If it's a decision that can easily be reversed, then I don't weigh in too heavily; it doesn't matter much, as you can change direction later. On the other hand, if you're set on robbing a bank or donating a kidney, that's another matter. Those choices are irreversible. I'll be noticeably more vocal when we discuss permanent decisions. It's still your call, but I want you to think long and hard before you decide—there's no going back.

A few months ago, my son called to discuss health insurance options. He was weighing risk and cost as we explored his company plan's choices. I made sure to verbalize the advantages and disadvantages of each option. One plan was expensive but offered excellent coverage; another plan cost less but posed greater financial risk.

Since it was a decision that could be changed during the next enrollment cycle, I was careful not to favor one option over the other. It's his decision, not mine. If I praise one choice and criticize the others, I box him in. There's no room to maneuver. He must go against me to pick another option, which creates distance and disagreement between us.

If I must give advice, it's soft advice. I make sure to clarify that it's not wrong if he chooses something else. In this insurance discussion, my son asked which plan I would choose. I answered carefully: "I might go with this option, but I think the others have merit as well. It's not a permanent decision, so don't worry about it. With the options you've presented, you can't go too wrong."

When you share different viewpoints and troubleshoot options for their decision, you don't pin them down. They have room to maneuver, to make their own choice.

If you give advice, your goal is to offer it without raising the disagreement bar too high. Make it easy for them to choose differently, without believing their choice will upset you.

Put it in the sandbox

Sometimes we view contrarian ideas with a hairy eyeball. We're skeptical, unsure whether to believe them. I propose putting those contrarian ideas into a sandbox. A sandbox is an isolated system for testing new procedures and ideas without risking failure in operations. When testing a new product, it goes in a laboratory—a sandbox. If I'm testing a new water valve for a purification plant, the first test isn't in the actual plant. It's in a test scenario—a sandbox.

- If the idea goes in the sandbox and doesn't work, it never comes out; it dies there.
- If it survives and thrives, bring it out and incorporate it into everyday life.

Let's consider opposing opinions using the sandbox concept. Suspend judgment and hold space for different ideas as you hear them.

A great example is the living wage. A friend introduced me to the idea about a year ago. He believes in it and explained it well, but I'm still a capitalist by nature. I'm still grappling with it, but I *am* thinking about it. It remains in the sandbox.

Bottom line: suspend judgment and remain curious.

As we close this chapter, remember that your ability to suspend judgment and remain curious will positively affect your conversations. This spirit of open engagement attracts people who want to be seen and heard for who they are. However, it's becoming more elusive as society continues toward shorter attention spans, self-elevation, and asynchronous communication.

CHAPTER 4

What Would I See?

*You can tell a great conversation by the way people
lean in, nod, and smile; engagement is visible.*
—Unknown

As a military aviator, I received a scheduled in-flight evaluation about every fifteen months; occasionally, I would get a no-notice evaluation in between. We called them check rides, and the evaluator had grading criteria to help determine whether the flight was a pass or fail.

The evaluator and I would sit down for a debrief after the flight ended. During the debrief, he would describe the mission and his observations. As he worked through the grading process, some areas had clear, well-defined grading criteria, while other parts of the mission had fuzzy criteria that could go either way at the evaluator's discretion.

This debrief was generally a mix of routine observations, evaluation feedback, and instruction. I learned something every time. During our conversation, I always took notes—I wrote down everything that was said, regardless of whether I agreed with the evaluator. I took extensive notes because I wanted to remember what was said; if they mentioned it, it must have been important.

Taking notes had another benefit: it sent a signal to the evaluator. I wanted them to see me writing down their comments. I wanted them to know I was genuinely listening. Taking notes sent that signal loud and clear; besides, I might get another evaluation from them later, and I didn't want them to think I didn't care.

The same thing happened if I flew with an instructor—there was always something to learn, and I approached these debriefs with the same mindset. I took a plethora of notes; it means a lot.

My point is this: take notes. Write something down. Early in my career, I learned to always bring something to write on for a check ride debrief. It sends a strong signal that I'm listening—truly listening. It's a habit that has served me well in connection and conversation.

WHAT WE CAN SEE

We judge others by their actions—what we can see, what they're doing. However, we judge ourselves by our intentions—what we mean to do. The issue is, I can't see what you're thinking; I can only see what you're doing. It helps to show people what we're thinking, to be obvious about it.

We judge others by their actions, but we judge ourselves by our intentions.

What you can see is key. That's why it was so important for the evaluator to see me writing down his feedback; I'm picking up what he's putting down, but taking notes makes it visible.

I'll share a personal example. We have a security system at our house, and I turn it on every night. Sometimes I leave early, so I must turn it off. After I leave, my intention is always to turn it back on, but sometimes I forget. It's rare, but it happens.

The other day, my wife mentioned, "I know you're leaving early tomorrow, so be sure to turn on the security system after you leave." At first, I thought, I know what to do; I always mean to turn it on, and most of the time I do. There's no reason to remind me. But I soon realized that my actions didn't always match my intentions. My intentions were good, but my follow-through was not where it needed to be. I judged myself by my intentions—meaning to turn it on—and she judged me by my actions—not always turning it on. Ultimately, it's not what we think that matters; it's what others see. Her reality was that I didn't always remember, and she wanted me to turn it on.

Don't multitask

You know what it is; we've all done it. You're in a virtual meeting, also working through email. The concept sounds good, but research shows it doesn't work. You split your attention between two things, giving your focus to one or the other, but not both. The result is that you're not effective at either.

The same happens in conversation. Multitasking and great interpersonal skills don't go together. When I see someone looking at their phone or typing on a computer, I sense a barrier, even if they don't. It signals that something else is more important. Personally, I shut down. I won't even try to compete. If it's not worth it to you, it's not worth it to me.

Here is the impact of multitasking: I was leading a workshop of about fifteen people, mostly front-line supervisors. Two of them in the front row worked for the same boss, a person I knew well. He was a good person and had the best of intentions. But as I overheard their conversation, their words were tough to hear. They said, "I wish my boss would listen to me. He's multitasking and doesn't even hear what I'm saying."

I wish my boss would listen to me. He's multitasking and doesn't even hear what I'm saying.

If you're a multitasker in conversation, you need to break that habit. Your conversations won't move the needle. It doesn't work when I'm one of several things you're doing at the same time.

Focus on the other

Make the conversation about them. Few people are willing and intentional enough to set themselves aside and be fully present for the other person. There's something special that happens when you focus on another person's needs, not your own. It's so uncommon that people notice, certainly subconsciously and often consciously. This outward focus naturally appears in your body language—it is something you can see.

LEARN HOW TO PLAY BALL

Talking with someone is like tossing a football back and forth: you throw them the ball by asking a question; they talk, then throw the ball back so you can speak. That's how it *should* work.

Sometimes you throw the ball to someone, and they just keep it—they keep talking. You rarely get the ball back; if you do, it's not for long.

Others catch the ball, hold it while they talk about themselves, then throw the ball on the ground. They don't ask you anything; they just stop, and things get quiet. You bend over and pick up the ball, ask another question, and throw the ball back to them. They talk about themselves for a bit, stop, and throw the ball on the ground again. Silence returns.

The same happens when you ask a question and get a one-word answer. You ask another, and get another brief reply. They're tossing the ball on the ground again.

The whole time, I think, Come on, this isn't how the game is played. It's exhausting, frustrating, and disappointing, because there could be so much more. The conversation could be far richer. When you do find someone who can really play ball, it's such a relief—and honestly, it's fun.

A great conversation is more of a collaborative event than a one-way street.

THEY'RE DEEP IN THOUGHT

You know what that looks like; we've discussed it already. They get quiet and stare, with a distant look. When you see that, you know they're on the journey, deep in thought. You might hear a soft sound—hmm or something like that. That's when you know.

These are signs that something good is coming down the pike. Don't rush in with a word suggestion or comment. Maybe they're trying to figure out how they feel about something; maybe it's a topic they haven't considered deeply. Give them the space to think. Let the silence be.

Listen well: People say the most wonderful things

At the end of that deep-in-thought look, you might hear something profound. When I'm talking with people, they say remarkable things—in ways I hadn't considered, with ideas I'd never explored, and words I might not have chosen. You'll observe this often if you're looking for it.

When I hear that "something powerful," I respond, "I like the way you said that." It lets them know I noticed and thought it was interesting. By the way, I never fake this—I'm a truth teller, so I don't pretend. They would see through it anyway; people are perceptive. I don't say it if I don't mean it.

When they do, capture it

Sometimes people have lightbulb moments—a significant thought materializes in front of them. These moments are unexpected and powerful, like a lightning strike. They might recognize the significance of their words, but more often it passes by; they say big things without noticing. When I repeat their statement to them, I often hear, "Wow. I said that?" I want to stop and linger at their statement.

I was working with a coaching client who had a breakthrough at one point—a powerful moment. (Side note: it's a privilege to be present when this happens.) I replied, "That was really powerful. Did you hear what you just said?" He came back with, "No, what did I say?"

Because I'm focused and listening, I felt the significance of it. I said, "I heard you, and I wrote it down. Here is what you just said: ___."

I always read it back exactly as it was said: same feelings, same words, same inflection. Their words are more powerful than mine, so I never paraphrase. When you point things out like this, it's a twofer: you capitalize on a breakthrough and create an intentional moment of connection. You're also giving them your gravitas (more on that later).

After repeating his statement back to him, I added, "Let's write that down." You already know I'm a fan of writing things down.

Writing things down causes it to land in a different place in your head. It sinks in deeper, stays longer, and helps you remember better.

I could tell he didn't immediately see the value of writing it down. He hesitated but then did it anyway, scribbling it on a piece of paper nearby. Then something interesting happened: he got quiet, staring at his own words. I waited, also quiet; I gave him room to maneuver.

He continued staring at the note, reading the words he had spoken only moments before but not realizing their significance. After a while, he looked up with a thoughtful, serious expression and said, "You know, when you write it down, it gets real." I agreed.

When you write it down, it gets real.

These words people speak—these lightning-strike moments—don't happen often. You have to watch for them: they hang in the air like smoke, like your breath on a cold January morning. They dissipate quickly when we move to the next set of words. If you don't capture the moment, their words disappear and their impact is gone. I try to live by the motto *carpe verba* (seize the words), and you should as well. Listen for their words, and seize them. Don't let them dissipate.

Carpe verba: seize the words.

What Would I See?

I was leading a workshop with a small group. In my workshops, I refuse to let anyone sit quietly; I'll draw something out of you during our time. I was writing on a flip chart with my back to the crowd when I heard a participant say, "I think my fear of delegation is holding back my team."

Even as I was writing something completely different on the flip chart, midword and midsentence, I heard those words and felt the emotion in them. The participant continued with another sentence. I stopped writing, immediately turned around, and said, "Hold on a second—don't say another word." I went over to a nearby whiteboard and wrote that sentence down. I knew if I let them continue to talk, I would forget their exact words. One sentence later, and those words would be gone—like smoke.

I couldn't let such a powerful statement go unnoticed; I had to stop and admire it. A moment like that doesn't happen often, and when it does, you simply must stop there for a moment. These moments are pearls of clarity that appear because we're having a good discussion, drawing them out. We're asking questions and truly listening—keenly listening—and here it comes. These are the things that make connection; it shows the other person we're truly listening. We're not thinking about lunch, what we're going to say, all the things we have to do, or anything else. We're all here, hearing everything you're saying. These are powerful moments that must be recognized when they come along.

Pause at these epiphanies, these powerful things. If you don't stop and marvel, you'll miss the moment, because they fade so fast.

THE MAGIC OF HANDWRITING

There's something magical about handwriting. We don't see as much handwriting these days, but there's something about it. When I write notes as people speak, I retain the information longer; it lands in a different place in my head, and sinks in deeper. Handwriting involves another part of your brain. The more places I have it as a memory, the better it sticks. The synthesis that occurs when editing your thoughts into words is a rewarding journey.

Make notes about your conversations to help you remember the details. Before you meet with them again, review your notes from the previous meeting. Even with the best of intentions, you can't remember everything. It makes a strong impact on the other person when you can recall their children's names and significant events in their lives.

ALWAYS HAVE SOMETHING TO WRITE ON

Remember the check ride story at the beginning of this chapter? I've also seen this in workshops as a speaker. When I say something and then see a participant writing it down, it's powerful feedback for me. It tells me they're listening, and what I'm saying is resonating with them.

Let's take that concept into the workplace. I've been in meetings and workshops when the senior leader comes to talk to the group and share some of their wisdom. Most people are attentive, but if you want to up your game, take notes. Write a few things down while they're talking. It helps you remember what they said and sends a strong signal to the speaker. Trust me: they notice who's writing it down.

During my time as an Air Force officer leading the executive suite, I've been that senior leader in the room, talking to a group for thirty minutes about all kinds of topics. My time is valuable, and I prepare comments and practice my delivery for the engagement. These are important things I want people to know and remember. Most of the time, I notice that about 90 percent aren't writing *anything* down. I know they can't remember all I'm saying. The 10 percent who are taking notes? I notice.

When you write things down, you tell the speaker you're listening and you recognize the importance of their words, words important enough to write down. It sends a signal, Lima Charlie. *Lima Charlie* is Air Force lingo for "I hear you Loud and Clear."

Please write this down, or at least act like it.
It helps me so much.
—Brady Cooper

It sends the same signal in a one-on-one conversation. It's an unspoken way to say what they just said is important. Their words are worthy of being written down and remembered. I always try to learn something from others; writing it down helps me remember it. When someone says something impactful or meaningful, I say, "That's good; I like the way you said that." Then I write it down. Many people miss an opportunity for better connection by not taking notes; they also forget most of the memorable things people say. Taking notes is a great way to show you're all in. Remember, others judge us by the actions they see, not by what we're thinking. Be intentional; be obvious. They'll notice.

Write things down during your conversation, then fill in missing information soon afterward. As I write, I say, "I tend to forget things like this if I don't write them down." Many people have the same issue; that makes you like everyone else. It also lets them know you think this part of their life is important enough to remember. These things help with connection.

More reasons to write

I often see people on their laptops in meetings. I don't know what they're doing. Even when they tell me they're taking notes, I look at them with a hairy eyeball, somewhat skeptical. Even when the meeting gets boring—which it will in about five minutes—you're all in, right?

Your coworkers also have an issue with what it looks like. When you use your computer to take notes during a conversation, it looks like you're surfing the internet. Even if you're not multitasking, it looks like you are. Even when you say, "I'm taking notes of our conversation on my computer." It just doesn't work as well. Most people know this already, but that doesn't seem to stop them from doing it.

You may have what seems like a good reason. "I can type much faster than I can write." The problem is, others won't buy it. It doesn't resonate. It doesn't look like you're listening; it just looks like you're working on something else. It puts up a barrier that inhibits connection.

Even if you're taking notes, research tells us that we don't retain things as well when we use a computer versus pen and paper. A 2014 study published in the *Association of Psychological Science* found that laptop notetakers tended to transcribe lectures verbatim rather than processing information and reframing it in their own words. This was detrimental to both long-term retention and understanding of the material.

You can certainly capture more data with a keyboard, but it goes in through the ears and right out through the fingertips—it doesn't stop anywhere along the way. You're better off spending your time listening than trying to capture every detail.

When we write, we reframe the words. We condense them so we can keep up. "Scrunch" is a word I used growing up; it means to make smaller. When we scrunch someone's spoken words into fewer written words, we synthesize them and remember them better. They sink in a different place in our head, and sink in deeper. This also forces us to be choosy about what to write, focusing on the most important things.

I hear all your reasons, but the bottom line is this: using your computer during conversations will negatively impact those conversations. It's something to consider.

CHAPTER 5

Environment and Body Language

—⚘—

*Friends are those rare people who ask how we
are, and then wait to hear the answer.*
—Ed Cunningham

As you would imagine, a lot of issues come up with 1,100 people under your command. You see things in people's lives that they would rather you not see, things they want to keep hidden. Not always bad things (although there were some), just sensitive things.

One morning, an Airman came into my office to have a serious discussion. He was what you would call a Marlboro man—tough on the exterior. It was a deep-end-of-the-pool conversation he didn't want to have but had to have because of what was going on.

It was a challenging personal situation, but he appeared to be keeping it together. Just what I expected. I could tell he was nervous, but I didn't realize how nervous until I saw his hands shaking ever so slightly, trembling with emotion. There was no mistaking it. I then noticed his voice—also a bit shaky. That told me the moment was close to his heart. I sat down in a chair next to him, just the two of us, and delicately proceeded.

As we talked, I could see him get misty eyed. Not a full-blown tear (he would never go there), but well on the way. These things, coming in rapid succession, drove home the fragility of the moment—the raw emotion that had to come out of this Marlboro man as he talked about his situation. If you saw this man out and about, or talked to him at work, you wouldn't expect this. He was a man's man, tough and rugged—he would never show weakness. But today, his armor was off and he was exposed.

When you find yourself in this place, watch for emotion and tread gently. Listen for their inflection as they speak. It's a sacred place not many get to see—a powerful display of emotion. Be honored you get to be present for it. Handle with care; a harsh approach in that moment will do a lot of damage that will take a long time, if ever, to repair or heal.

I almost messed it up. If you had told me I would see that body language in him, I'm not sure I would have believed it—but it was there. Noticing those small indicators allowed me to realize how significant our conversation was for him. Had I not seen that, I might have relied on my tough-guy perception and not handled it correctly.

You've seen how important body language is to the conversation. But environment plays a key part as well. Let's start with environment.

ENVIRONMENT

LOCATION
Some locations are just more conducive to a great conversation and connection. Let's say you're watching a three-year-old. Probably not the right time to get in the deep end of the pool with another adult. But a quiet setting when you have some availability would be perfect. These are things we intuitively know but tend to forget. For greater success, get the right location to set yourself up for better odds.

Let's identify our objectives so we can set ourselves up. What's the basis of the discussion? Is it formal or informal? Is there a disciplinary focus, or is it a casual conversation? The location is one of the first steps in setting the tone for any discussion.

A meeting in your office is different than a meeting in *their* office, which is different than a meeting in the break room, which is different than a meeting in the conference room, which is different than a meeting at the local coffee shop. You wouldn't have a serious conversation at a volleyball game, nor would you deliver a formal reprimand in a coffee shop. If you decide to have the meeting in your office, should you sit behind the desk or in a chair next to them? What vibe are you trying to convey? It all begins with objective. Changing the location of a discussion can dramatically change the engagement and the outcomes.

Create the environment that is most conducive to achieving your objective.

As you create that space, also think of barriers and body positioning. Removing physical barriers helps to remove the mental ones as well. If you want to close the distance, both physically and emotionally, don't put anything between the two of you. However, if barriers help you achieve your objective, then include them.

Some conversations are best held in person. You wouldn't have a serious conversation over text because you can't convey tone and body language. Some topics are best discussed over candlelight; others in a noisy bar. Some conversations can be asynchronous, whereas others need to be conducted in real time. For the best outcome, align the factors of mode and environment.

We are easily distracted

Focus is challenging. Remember all that unused cognitive space in our head? Your brain wants to be busy. It's looking for things to do. While you're listening to your friend talk about a troubled relationship, you're also watching a bird chase a tortilla chip near the table next to you. Distraction is everywhere. One way to prevent distraction is to think ahead and mitigate its impact.

Set yourself up for success. Place yourself in the room in a way that provides less distraction. One of my friends said that when he and his wife go to a restaurant, his wife sits in the seat where she can see the TV—not so she can watch it, but to keep him from watching it! She strategically chooses her seat because she knows he's easily distracted. She knows her objective and optimizes her environment for success.

Sometimes, instead of trying to aggressively ignore the distraction, we might choose to go upstream and change the input. That might mean sitting with your back to the crowd so they don't demand your attention.

I know that won't sit well with former law enforcement officers and special forces guys. They like to sit where they can see the crowd and the door; they want their back to the wall. (I like eating lunch with them because I know they'll see something develop long before I will.)

In the words of the great philosopher Clint Eastwood, a.k.a. Dirty Harry, "Man's got to know his limitations." I know I'm easily distracted, so I look for a seat facing the wall. My wife and I joke about this when we go to a restaurant. There's a lot of responsibility that comes with sitting with your back to the wall, so I'll remind her to be alert for any danger. She has to remain vigilant while I get to be completely carefree, eating my meal, unencumbered with that responsibility.

Man's got to know his limitations.
—Harry Callahan (Magnum Force, 1973)

WE'RE ALWAYS CONNECTED . . . UNFORTUNATELY

We live in an always-on world. Our pace is frenetically fast—but it's obviously not fast enough, because we're always looking for ways to make it faster, better, quicker. We hear people talking about a "digital detox," but there was a time in our not-too-distant past when that term didn't even exist.

Everyone cool is wearing a smart watch. Yes, they offer convenience; they're useful. A world of information on your wrist! However, they can be a distractor in conversation. At best, the buzzing on your wrist is a short mental diversion; at worst, a glance at it will make you appear distracted and disinterested. One look might not hurt, but it sends a strong signal if repeated. If you do wear a smart device, consider turning notifications off while engaging in important conversations.

Your phone is also a distractor. How many of us have been in conversation with someone who couldn't put their phone away for five minutes? I can't help but think, Why don't you put your phone away and talk to the real person in front of you instead of the virtual person on your phone? I become dramatically less engaged in our conversation. Putting your phone away serves two purposes: it keeps you from being distracted and it avoids distracting the other person.

Put your phone away somewhere so you can't hear it ring or feel it vibrate. Don't put it on the table, even face down. When you do that, you're sending the message that your phone is as important as the other person. Two's company, but three's a crowd.

As a military man, I've heard the phrase "Preparing the battlespace" for many years. At the beginning of Desert Storm in 1991, USAF F-117 stealth fighters prepared the battlespace by striking early warning radars in Iraq in advance of the main attack force. That enabled the main thrust to strike a blinded enemy. They were preparing the battlespace for success.

Let's say you're expecting an important call. The best thing is to lead with that before you ever begin the conversation: "I'm waiting for an important call from my doctor, so I may have to step aside to take a call during our conversation. I hope that's okay." No one would mind. This is how we prepare the battlespace for success.

Connecting Virtually

A lot of people complain that it's impossibly hard to connect in a virtual setting. They think you have to be in person, face to face, to really connect. It's a great excuse, but it doesn't hold water. Funny thing is, you do the same things in a virtual setting that you would in person. You just do them in different ways. There's nothing magic to it; it's just the environment that's different. Don't let a virtual engagement scare you—you can connect there just like anywhere else.

The fundamentals are the same. You've got to be real, authentic, engaging. Eye contact is still important. Remember to look at the camera and not the person so that it appears you're looking them in the eye. (By the way, it goes without saying that your camera is on. If eye contact is critical, having your camera turned off won't work.)

The fundamentals of a virtual connection are the same. We just display them differently.

We tend to talk with our hands when we're truly engaged, when we're really into it. In a virtual setting, get your hands going. Get them up so you can see them on the screen, which means the other person can see them as well. You're doing the same things, but in such a way that the camera can see it. You want the camera to see your body language.

—ɯ—

BODY LANGUAGE

My wife said something one time that really struck me: We taste things with our eyes first. She's exactly right. Food tastes better when it looks better. That's why we make fancy birthday cakes; they pop and make the occasion more special. The cake looks great, and the cake tastes great. It packs a bigger punch when we combine two senses.

Body language is like that. It tells so much about what's going on with a person. Humans are perceptive; we can listen with our ears and our eyes. Are you listening on all levels, ears and eyes? Does your body language match what you're saying? Your intention? We're going for a coordinated message, meaning all our signals match.

Make sure all parts of you are sending the same message.

Body language usually tells the truth. If I asked which one you would trust more, someone's words or their body language, you would probably say body language. I know I would. Facial expressions and gestures tend to convey true feelings, especially when several indicators point to the same thing. Trust is significantly shaped by nonverbal signals, and incongruent signals can lead to doubt or suspicion.[9]

I once spoke to a group where a person in the crowd fell asleep with his mouth open. I had to work hard to overcome that. Were they just tired, or was my message that boring? I had to actively choose the former as the latter would have derailed me completely.

If you've ever done any public speaking, you know how important body language is, both your own and the audience's. You can tell when the crowd is engaged and when they're not. Laughter after a joke is crucial. Applause at the right moment signals that a beat has landed.

So what signals are we sending as we engage with others? If you think what they said was funny but you don't laugh or make any outward gesture, how will they know? We have to be intentional about our engagement; I want the other person to know that I'm right there with them.

Effective body language can help convey what you're feeling in your heart as you listen. But don't fake it. If you do, they'll figure it out. We've all seen the "power pose" body language videos. They just seem fake.

---

[9] Simon and Mishra, *IJRPR*, April 2025.

I'm not saying they have zero merit, but it just works better when it's genuine.

Just like we taste food with our eyes before we eat it, we listen with our eyes and our ears. We hear what they're saying and compare it to what we're seeing.

Let's bring that idea into our conversations. Remember, it's a two-way street: Compare what you're seeing with what you're hearing, and compare what you're feeling with how you're showing it. Combine both senses for maximum impact and connection.

Eye contact is king

It goes without saying, but eye contact is king. Whenever I ask what makes a good listener, eye contact is always in the top three responses. It's so important—but you already knew that. Everyone already knows it, but we seem to forget it or ignore it. The eyes are the window to the soul. If you want to know where someone's attention is focused, look where they're looking.

Any number of things can cause us to break eye contact. We've talked briefly about our phones and smart watches, but there are others. For guys it might be a nice watch or a fast car or yoga pants. For women, maybe it's Matthew McConaughey in Wayfarers and a white V-neck T-shirt. There's way too much competition for our attention.

The uncomfortable stare

There's something magical about eye contact, but too much of a good thing just makes it weird. You might need to break the gaze. I once coached someone with an uncomfortable stare. Funny thing is, he wasn't aware of it.

I noticed it during our first session, and I hoped it was just a one-time thing. Nope—he did it again during the second session, so I knew I would have to say something. I was his leadership coach; if I didn't do it, no one would.

According to a 2016 article by the *British Psychological Study*, most people prefer eye contact of between two and five seconds. More than that, and it gets uncomfortable. Another study in *Scientific American* found that magic number to be precisely 3.2 seconds. These general rules are good for a Western society but may not work in other places, since eye contact norms can vary significantly across cultures.

Our next time together, I began this challenging conversation with "Can I be frank with you? Is it okay if I talk about something that might be kind of tough?" That was powerful, because it asked him to open the door so I could walk in with what might be tough feedback. It prepared the battlespace and increased the odds that he would truly receive something. He said yes, and the conversation went well. He was simply an engineer who also happened to be an overly intent listener. After our conversation, his eye contact started falling in the normal range—he heard my feedback and adjusted well. The bottom line is, eye contact is important during our conversations, but let's be careful not to overdo it.

Eye contact is important—but don't overdo it.

That "open the door" phrase was one I learned from a coworker many years ago. I was talking with him about an employee I was struggling with. I'd described all the wrong things the employee was doing, as well as all the right things they weren't doing. My coworker listened politely, then asked a powerful question: "Can I tell you something that might sting just a little?" Rather reluctantly, I said, "Well, I guess so. Sure."

He came right back with "Bad employee, bad supervisor."

Ouch. But he was right. Employees do exactly what you let them do. I wasn't holding my employee accountable, and their bad behavior was my fault. If he had simply blurted out those words ("Bad employee, bad supervisor"), I wouldn't have received the critique as well. He knew how to prepare the battlespace for success. He *asked* me to open the door instead of kicking it open. Smart move. I'd be a rich man if I had a nickel for every time I've repeated that story, because it's so helpful.

SOME GREAT BODY LANGUAGE

What about when we want them to know we're all in? You want to really listen and convey that feeling. You want it to be obvious, but it's a fine line. What behaviors would I see from someone who's all in? Let's start with these:

- Eye contact
- Verbal responses like *Mm-hmm, Oh yeah, Keep going,* and *Right on.*
- Leaning in when their voice gets low
- Nodding at the right times
- Taking notes when they say something powerful
- Repeating what they said, word for word ("You told him that his tie wasn't working for him? No way!")

I told you, all these things you already know. We just need to be reminded of them now and then. None of this stuff will be hard when you're not multitasking or distracted.

BE ANIMATED, EVEN IF IT'S JUST A BIT

Animation kicks it up a notch. The synergy of demonstrating engagement through words and visuals is a powerful connector. It reinforces the message you want to send.

- It might be hand gestures when someone says something amazing. You can send an "Oh my goodness!" signal without saying a word: cover your mouth with your hand and raise your eyebrows.
- You could put a hand on your chin to demonstrate intent listening.
- If someone says something powerful, it could be a fist bump.

You may also need to animate your voice. Nothing says boring like a deadpan, monotone response. Now, if that's your normal voice, it's a bit more challenging. You'll have to inject some pitch changes into your regular vocal cadence.

YOU NEED A POKER FACE

Animation can help in conversation, but we also have to be careful about our expressions. Microexpressions are those inadvertent facial expressions that can appear without warning or will. A great example of this is a genuine smile. When you can see their gums around their teeth, it's almost always a real smile. That kind of smile is hard to fake. Microexpressions are hard to control, but the good thing is they don't last long. Everything after that is controllable. That's why you have to learn to put on that poker face.

Sometimes people say something unexpected. Learn to be ready for that comment when it comes, and don't let facial insubordination get you. Pretend you're playing Texas Hold 'Em and put on that poker face. It's so important to listen without judgment because your thoughts will show in your facial expressions. Keep control of those emotions, and learn not to be surprised by anything. Fix your face.

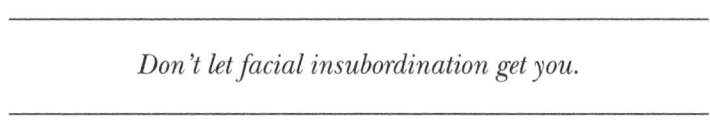

Don't let facial insubordination get you.

I was talking to a thirtysomething friend as she described an issue she was having with an employee. As we continued, she kept using the word "elderly" to describe her. Finally, after about the fourth time, I asked, "You keep using the word *elderly*. Just how old is this woman?" She replied, "Oh! My goodness. She's old! She's probably in her sixties."

I nodded and kept my poker face, and we kept talking. Behind my poker face, I grinned. I was less than two years from that age myself! I flattered myself that I must have looked young, but in reality, she was probably just a bad judge of age. She was also a kind soul who would never intentionally offend anyone. Another catastrophic loss of situational awareness! Some folks would call her on it, but I remembered my objective: connection and engagement. I let it go. Making an issue of it wouldn't have helped me achieve my objective.

LOOK FOR TELLS AND SIGNALS
I was leading a workshop one day, and one participant was talking to a coworker. "Oh, I can tell when you're done. You start to back up and walk away from the conversation when you're ready to move on." It was a light bulb moment for the other person, a gift of valuable feedback.

Ask yourself: "Do I have any tells when I check out of a conversation?" You might even ask your coworkers or close friends if they've ever seen them in you. I know a person who, when he's done talking, starts looking around the crowd. He no longer looks you in the eye. That's his tell, his signal, that as far as he's concerned, this conversation is finished.

Once you know your unconscious moves, they become conscious. Once you're aware of them, you get to make the decision when to roll them out. Sometimes you want to send the signal that it's time to end this conversation. For example, there's only a few times you can listen to a relative talk about his collection of cereal boxes from the 1970s. The key is to be intentional about it and roll out the right body language at the appropriate time.

We also look for tells in others. Often when I'm in conversation, I know when someone wants to say something. Maybe they take a breath or make some kind of noise; you might even see it on their face. When you see those signs, let them into the conversation. I'll quickly finish my sentence and then say, "Go ahead. You were getting ready to say something; what was it?"

FIDGETING IS DISTRACTING
Fidgety people can be distracting. If you tend to fidget, or play with a pen, your keys, or anything else, make it a point not to have those things anywhere nearby. A friend of mine was talking to a group, thinking it was going well. At the break, his assistant came up to him and yanked his pen out of his hand. He was surprised at the move until she told him, "You're

clicking that pen while you're talking, and it's driving me crazy! I'm not hearing anything you're saying!" He didn't even realize how distracting it was. Now he makes a point to not have a clicky pen nearby when he's engaged in a conversation, speaking, or in other places where it might be distracting. It certainly felt natural to him, but it wasn't helping the connection.

Don't look at the clock

I know I'm telling you to be completely engaged in the conversation. When you're all in, you would never look at your watch in the middle of their sentence. That sends a pretty strong signal of "I'm ready to move on." However, we're all limited and bound by time. We all have appointments, obligations, and places to be that are just as important as this conversation, and we don't want to be late.

A few options can help us keep up with the time during conversations. One way is to sit where you can see a clock on the wall. I was talking to a friend who told me he kept a clock under his desk, where only he could see it. That way he could look at it without the other person knowing it.

My favorite, my go-to, is one I use all the time when I'm talking to someone. While the other person is talking, they'll likely be moving their hands around. When their hands come up in my field of view, I look at their watch to keep up with the time. Besides, I don't want to stare into their eyes the whole time—we've already talked about the uncomfortable gaze!

When we're talking, I look at your watch to see what time it is.

I want to be engaged in the conversation, but perhaps I have an appointment in twenty minutes that I can't miss. Both our conversation and my upcoming appointment are important, and I need to keep track of the time. I never want someone to think that I'm impatient for our conversation to end, but I've also got other things going on as well. I'll look at my own watch as a last resort, but I try to glance at theirs if I can.

Take your sunglasses off

If the eyes are the window to the soul, then sunglasses pull the shades on that window. Never wear sunglasses in a conversation, especially mirrored ones. They worked well for Maverick, and you might think they're stylish, but they're a brick wall when it comes to connection. You would never cover your eyes during a conversation, but that's the effect sunglasses have. Eye contact is essential, and it's a significant barrier to connection when I can't see your eyes.

Sunglasses can also be intimidating: they convey a sense of superiority. While working as a security guard, it's probably acceptable to wear sunglasses. If that's the message you want to send, go for it. While performing security duties, you're probably not trying to connect or have a real conversation with anyone anyway. You're scanning for threats—a different objective. However, if you want to make a genuine connection, sunglasses get in the way.

When you're on the phone

We've already said there are three parts to communication: words, tone, and body language. When you're on the phone, there's no body language; your voice and tone have to pick up the slack to compensate. You want to unmistakably convey that you're present with them in the story. That might include more verbal comments. If you were in person, you would use your facial expressions to connect. Put that same feeling into your voice. Add expression and animation, and use verbal body language that reflects your emotions in the moment.

Physical touch

I was talking with a man over coffee as he described a situation. He touched me on the arm at just the right moment, and it gave me goosebumps. It was a powerful reminder of the impact of touch: there's something powerful about human touch, and we all intuitively know it. If you mean it and want to get someone's attention, touch them on the arm or the shoulder—but only if it's appropriate. Don't go farther than the shoulder, and don't fake it; if you fake it, they'll see through it.

As a C-130 crewmember, we used checklists to help us complete the myriad tasks that had to be done in the right order at the right time. There were checklists for Before Taxi, After Takeoff, Combat Entry, and Before Landing, among others. The flight engineer ran the checklists with a call-and-response cadence: they would call out the checklist item, and the crewmember who did it would say "Checked" or "Complete." When the entire checklist was complete, the flight engineer would firmly grasp each pilot on the shoulder and say, "After Takeoff checklist complete." There was so much going on that it was easy for the pilots to become distracted. The touch on the shoulder was a highly effective, nonverbal way to draw their attention to this important fact.

I hope you see how important environment and body language can be to an effective conversation. Think about which technique or tool you can use during your next one. I suggest you choose one that comes naturally; it'll be easier to adopt and more authentic in its implementation.

CHAPTER 6

The Words You Use

*The right word at the right time will unlock the door
to treasures—the wrong one will close it forever.*
—Rasheed Ogunlaru

ONE OF MY FRIENDS IS a trained hostage negotiator. He's been in several difficult situations. Sometimes it was an actual hostage event; other times, a barricaded person or someone experiencing suicidal thoughts. I was curious about what it takes to succeed in such a role, so I asked him to lunch to hear his stories.

He began with a statement that might surprise some people: "Everybody thinks that, when you're a hostage negotiator, you're supposed to talk all the time. The biggest thing they teach you is to be a good listener and keep your mouth shut."

A great negotiator gets them talking, then listens.

Once the conversation is underway, stay quiet and let them talk—words of wisdom we should all learn from. Listen carefully and search for common ground. Once you find it, they open up, and you can start to engage. Their feelings will start to surface, and then you can move forward. By listening, you discover their real issues.

He also stressed the importance of empathy—being able to put yourself in another's place. There is, however, a pitfall to avoid, a line you must never cross. "You never say, 'I know how you feel,' because you'll hear, 'You don't know how I feel.' Instead, say something like, 'I've never been through that before; tell me about it.'" Don't assume you know what's happening in their world or exactly how they feel.

Again and again, he emphasized the value of silence. "When there's silence, most people just want to fill the space." He would often let silence become uncomfortable, and the other person would begin speaking to fill the space.

Like a hostage negotiator, the words you choose are crucial—equally important are the words you don't use. How you leverage silence, maintain tactical patience, listen, and respond after a pause are all integral to a meaningful conversation.

Verbal Judo

Verbal judo is a term I hear mostly from police officers. It describes the use of words and tone to de-escalate a situation. Officers aim to resolve every situation at the lowest possible level of confrontation, and they use verbal judo to achieve that. It's all about the words, tone, and timing. When it all comes together, it's impressive.

I used to work with a man named Mark. He had such a way with words—a black belt in verbal judo. Mark was the guy who could sell two bags of ice to someone in Alaska. He once chastised me (deservedly), but, afterward, I was smiling and thanking him as he left my office. He taught me about verbal judo, though I never achieved his level of skill. Mark, a former police officer, often shared remarkable stories about the difficult situations he found himself in. Police officers tell some of the best stories, and he was no exception. His verbal judo was unparalleled.

Remember the term verbal judo. You don't need to reach black-belt status, but the right words at the right moment can be very powerful.

The Words You Use

LET'S SLOW IT DOWN

The Royal International Air Tattoo is an air show in England where hundreds of airplanes from around the world gather for a weekend. Several hundred thousand people come out to see the show; it's quite a sight if you enjoy aviation. One year, our C-130 unit was invited. I actually sat on top of the airplane and watched the many aerobatic performances. It was an unforgettable experience.

As you might imagine, the event had robust security. I spent time with the guard that kept watch around our airplane. He was from Scotland, and I enjoyed his unique expressions, but he was a fast talker! His thick accent made connection challenging. Most of the time, I was three or four words behind, struggling to keep up. Maintaining the pace required all my concentration.

The lesson: If you're talking to someone for whom English isn't a first language, slow down. If you have a strong accent, slow down. Cultural and linguistic barriers can impede connection; sometimes, you must be intentional about slowing your speech.

STICK WITH EVERYDAY WORDS

Barriers arise through our choice of words. If I use language you don't understand, you might miss my point. Once, in a group book study, a friend commented that the discussion guide contained questions with rare and unfamiliar words. My friend sensed the author was trying to impress readers with their vocabulary.

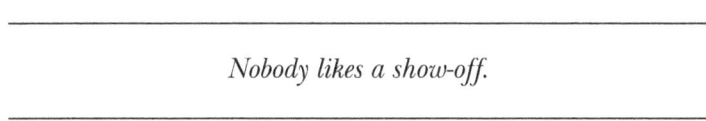

Nobody likes a show-off.

Avoid using unusual or uncommon words in conversation—most people won't know them. This isn't a spelling bee or a dictionary lesson. I'm thinking of words like *celerity, pugnacious, ebullient,* and *cacophony*. These only obfuscate the message (*obfuscate*: to make unclear or confusing; an uncommon word used intentionally). At best, large words are distracting; at worst, they're a barrier to connection. Most people sense that you're trying to impress with your vocabulary, creating unnecessary distance. Whether speaking or writing, elaborate language tends to alienate an audience.

Pause to slow down the conversation

Pause and consider your words before you speak. If someone says something insightful or meaningful, respond with a thoughtful "Hmm . . ." Use clear body language and facial expressions to show you're processing their words and formulating a considered reply. This can create a sense of anticipation, leading to deeper connection.

Hold the space with a thoughtful pause.

A friend once used a vivid metaphor to illustrate this kind of pause. Imagine you're in the late 1700s, dressed like Benjamin Franklin. Everyone back then smoked a pipe. When someone says something you would normally respond to, you put your pipe in your mouth, take a long draw, and then exhale. Smoke is flying all over the place. Only then do you reply. In conversation, imagine holding a pipe and taking a draw to create space for thought.

Please don't fake any of this. I pause intentionally to foster connection, because I'm genuinely interested in the other person and want them to know it. I try not to plan my reply while they're still speaking. My pause is sincere—I'm truly thinking of my response. If you try to fake it, the exchange will go terribly sideways. Don't do it.

Being disinterested is bad, but being disingenuous is far worse.

This pause between their comment and your reply—a moment of quiet—is rare in most conversations. Many people rush through discussion; set yourself apart by being intentional. This deliberate pause signals that you're not in a hurry and gives both parties room to maneuver.

Use their words, not yours

People say insightful things. They also say them in ways I wouldn't think of, using different words. Their words are powerful in both content and delivery.

Once, in a small workshop setting, a participant said, "People want to sell on facts and logic, but everyone buys on emotion." He was a salesperson, and his delivery showed that he knew what he was talking about. I recognized the power of his words and wrote them on the whiteboard exactly as he said them.

We lightly touched this earlier, but let's dig in deeper for a moment. Repeating their words is a powerful connector. If you must paraphrase, ask permission and use as many of their words as possible.

Don't paraphrase; use their words every chance you get.

There are several good reasons to use their words in conversation.

- Their words are more meaningful to them than your words are. Your words may be really good and resonate with them, but their words resonate more. Remember it's about them, not you. When you paraphrase, you're telling them that you can come up with better words to describe their feeling than they can.
- When you use their words, you demonstrate, "I'm listening to you. I'm present." This conveys undivided attention. If you weren't listening intently, you wouldn't be able to repeat their words.

- You show that you value their words when you repeat them. You're giving them your gravitas. I often say, "I love the way you said that." And I mean it. I'm a truth teller; if I don't mean it, I won't say it.
- Sometimes, I'll say, "I gotta write that down." When I do, it lets them know I'm learning from them. There's always something to learn. Writing it down is another way to show appreciation and help you remember.
- When you repeat their words, they can clarify or provide more context. Maybe you misheard or misunderstood. They get to jump back into the conversation to add more background and information.
- When you paraphrase, you risk misinterpretation. You might say something that offends them. We've all heard "No, that's not what I said! What I meant was . . ." as they repeat themselves. We want to avoid this because it doesn't help us connect. Use their words to reflect what was said. Miscommunication is common, and paraphrasing increases the risk of error.
- It's especially engaging when someone uses an uncommon word. For instance, *paragon* means "an excellent example of something." A great follow-up would be this: "*Paragon* . . . that's an interesting word. Tell me how you chose it." This leads to deeper discussion.

How to honor their words

When you repeat their words, also mirror the inflection they used. This further demonstrates you were really listening. It reflects the emotions present in their tone, which they may not realize.

When you have echoed their words, close with a confirming question:

- So, I just heard you say, "_____." Is that correct?
- So, "_____." That's seems like a big statement. Walk me through how you got there.
- You said, "_____." Is that a good summary?
- You said, "_____." Is that a fair characterization?

SCRUNCH THAT DOWN FOR ME

When I facilitate workshops, I sometimes ask leaders to share their biggest challenge. I favor this question for many reasons; a principal reason is that they often discover their challenges are the same as other leaders. When I ask, I frequently receive rambling, thirty-second answers. One of my goals is to record their exact words on a flip chart, but I can't transcribe everything—there's not enough room, and I can't write that fast. Remember, we don't paraphrase.

If someone uses a lot of words, it's powerful to ask a clarifying question: "How would I capture what you just said in a short sentence?" Or "Give that to me in a short phrase." Or "Give that to me in a brief phrase." Sometimes I say, "Scrunch all that down into ten words or less, so I can write it on this flip chart." Scrunch is a southern word to use every chance you can.

They get a thoughtful look, and I wait. I'm never in a hurry here. That scrunch question takes them on a mental journey, tightening their thoughts. It forces them to synthesize and compress their words into a concise, more powerful statement. It often brings clarity because they must select the most impactful words to capture their thoughts.

I want them on that journey. The process of distilling thoughts into a short, power-packed sentence is worthwhile.

I would have written you a shorter letter if
I'd only had more time.
—Mark Twain

It takes mental effort to reduce twenty-five words to ten. It's easy to toss words around in conversation; it's much more challenging to be intentional and concise in word choice.

It takes effort to scrunch, which is exactly what I'm after. These actions encourage connection; they stand out and help you become rare and memorable, like Nate.

When you get feedback

There are only two words to remember when you receive feedback: thank you. Say it, and mean it. Even if you don't agree or are unsure, say thank you anyway. Even when it stings, say thank you.

The only words you say when you receive feedback are "Thank you."

Reply with something simple and genuine: "Thank you for saying that. I know it was tough to tell me, and it took moral courage. I appreciate your candor." Responses like these keep the feedback loop open.

Anything other than thank you tends to shut people down. Don't try to explain your reasoning or rationale. This sounds like, "Yes, I hear you, but you don't understand . . ." Your explanation will likely fall on deaf ears. This response decreases your likelihood of more feedback from them in the future.

Shooting the messenger is another sure way to shut the feedback door. It discourages further feedback; next time, they'll take the easy road and remain silent. You won't hear from them anymore, even when you need it. Your goal is to keep the door open to feedback. No one wants to be the emperor with no clothes.

The smooth compliment

When you compliment someone, it can create an awkward moment. It sounds like, "Hey, I heard you were promoted—congratulations!" There's a thank-you and then an awkward silence. They're unsure how to respond. I've been there on both sides, and it *is* awkward.

Here's an idea: add a question after the compliment. It makes responding easier and keeps the conversation moving. It provides an easy conversational path forward. It goes something like this: "Congrats on the promotion!" And then you follow with up with one of these questions:

- "When do you start your new role?"
- "What are some of the challenges you expect in your new role?"
- "How soon will you be able to transition your responsibilities from your previous position?"

These questions allow them to acknowledge the compliment and move past the awkward stage. They remove friction and light the path for the conversation to move forward.

Ask them, and they'll open the door

Asking permission to suggest another viewpoint invites them to open the door for you to offer it; it's rare for someone to refuse, and it dramatically increases the likelihood of your words being received. Gaining permission prepares their mental space for your perspective. It might sound like, "I hear what you're saying. May I offer a different perspective?" It's like plowing the field before planting corn: it simply grows better.

Plow the field before you plant the seed.

The ask opens their mind to be more receptive; suggesting a different perspective without first asking permission is like kicking the door open, and it's not received as well as when you knock.

This also works if you want to tell a story. It's another way to prepare the conversational space. It opens up the other person's mind and focuses their attention. The story tends to land better. It might sound like, "Can I share a story? I think it could help."

What's in a name?

When you meet someone or start a conversation, how do you remember their name? Do you repeat it in your head, repeat it aloud, or write it down? What's your preferred technique?

> *Remember that a person's name is to that person the sweetest and most important sound in any language.*
> —Dale Carnegie

Many people struggle with remembering names. When the elephant is in the room, we all see it; we all know it's there. The best thing is to point to it and address it. Let's acknowledge this challenge. Make a thing out of it. When you're overt and intentional about remembering names, it signals that you care.

I've tried several approaches to name memorization, but repeating their name as you shake their hand can help. You could also use their name in conversation to reinforce it.

I was leading a workshop at a client site and met a capable young man named Nicholas. Always seeking ways to remember names, I said, "Great to meet you, Nicholas. It is Nicholas, isn't it? Do you prefer Nicholas or Nick? I want to make sure I get that right."

These actions make you rare and memorable. I'm being intentional, and I want him to know that I care enough to get his name right and in the way he prefers. Notice that I said his name four times in that exchange. This also helps me remember it.

I've met folks named Steven who don't want to be called Steve. I met a man named Michael who preferred Mike. If her name is Rebecca, don't assume she's comfortable with Becky. Maybe only her mother uses that name. You never know unless you ask. In asking, you display intentionality and care, which makes you stand out.

If I'm unsure about a name, I ask, "Did I say your name correctly?" If I messed it up, I'll thank them for correcting me. You want to remember and pronounce their name correctly during conversation. Again, their name is the sweetest sound they'll hear, so let's get it right.

Sometimes I use the technique of spelling the name back to them, especially when it's unique or could be spelled in different ways. If someone introduced herself as Cathy, I would ask, "Is that with a *C* or a *K*?

Does it end in 'y' or 'i'?" This further cements the name in my mind. It also signals that I think her name is important enough to get it right. It doesn't help to send an email and misspell her name!

If you can write their name down, it's a game changer. Recording it further demonstrates your intent to remember it. It's that important, so I take the time to write it down. Writing also helps with memory.

It doesn't matter what technique you use, as long as it works. Do what you must, but let them hear the message Lima Charlie, loud and clear: I care enough to get your name right.

Remember, you're investing in them mentally and emotionally—all these actions send a clear signal. I want to invest in them, and I want them to know I'm investing. If you care about someone but never say so, it doesn't have the same effect. You want them to know, without stating it outright. These are overt ways for them to recognize that.

I was listening to the podcast "Making Masters of the Air," about the HBO miniseries. They discussed Captain "Rosie" Rosenthal. If you've seen the series, you know he was a powerful figure in the 100th Bomb Group. The men connected with Rosie. The podcast said, "Guys listened to [Rosie] because he didn't pontificate . . . He put you at ease immediately." He didn't force his opinions and ideas. You know what it's like being around people who pontificate: they forcefully offer their opinion in a haughty manner and expect you to agree. A little of that goes a long way; it gets old quickly.

WHEN YOU FORGET THEIR NAME

Recently I ran into someone I'd worked with several years ago, but I couldn't remember their name. The whole time we were talking, I was trying to think of it. Remember, the brain thinks faster than people talk, and we've all got cognitive room that is ripe for distraction. The whole time we were talking, I was listening with one half of my brain and trying to remember his name with the other half.

The lesson here: if you're with someone you haven't seen in a while, maybe someone you don't know very well, reintroduce yourself. Assume they don't know or remember your name. Most people who don't remember your name simply won't ask. They'll fake it and maybe think of it two days later at best.

Begin the conversation with "Hey, great to see you again! It's been a minute, hasn't it? I'm Keith. Tell me your name again? I can be terrible with names." This either confirms what they thought your name was, or it tells them again if they completely forgot. Either way, they're not struggling to remember it as you talk. It's just one less thing for them to be distracted by. You want to make your conversation as easy as possible, and this is another way to do that.

Most of us remember faces, but the names don't stick as well. But most people have been there before, and they appreciate the honesty. If they seem offended that you couldn't remember them, just come back with, "I'm good with faces but not great at remembering names. It's something I'm working on, and I appreciate your understanding." Genuineness and authenticity are interpersonal qualities that supercharge connection.

Humor

Sometimes, it's just not the time for humor. Some people have a habit of saying something funny to lighten the mood; however, there are times when the mood needs to remain as it is. It could be a serious topic, where someone needs to get something off their chest. A lame attempt at humor at that moment may sound tone-deaf or break the moment. The more appropriate action would be to sit in a posture of quiet, active listening.

When a funny comment comes to mind, pause for a few seconds.

- Will it add to or detract from the moment?
- Will it sound as if you're not taking them seriously?
- Is it a topic where humor is inappropriate, or only marginally appropriate?

Those answers will help you decide whether to share that comment or keep it to yourself.

Set boundaries if you need to

Sometimes, you need to set boundaries on the conversation. This sounds as simple as, "I want to hear about this, but I've only got about five minutes until my next event—so give me the abbreviated version." It's up to you whether you stick to your guns and walk away when five minutes are up. Some people won't take the hint; be prepared to follow through. This is especially helpful when working with an energy vampire or someone with little self-awareness.

Lob the softball over the plate

Most people love to tell stories. A great way to get someone talking is to ask a question that sets them up to tell a story. Say something like, "That sounds fascinating. How did you figure that out?" Or "Tell me about your journey from Kroger cart wrangler to cybersecurity engineer. That sounds wild!" Lob the softball question over the plate, then step back and watch them hit it out of the park. Then do it again. When you do, you'll discover many interesting things about people.

I've led and participated in over one thousand job interviews. At the end of each interview, I gave them the softball question: "That's all the questions we have. Is there anything else before we wrap up?" That was my way of giving them the floor, hoping they would drive home their strong points. I wanted them to tell me why they deserved the position.

This was my way to lob the softball over the plate. I hoped they would hit it out of the park. The softball question was nice and slow, right in the strike zone. However, more often than not, they would have nothing to add. They figuratively stood at the plate while the ball floated by, bat resting on their shoulder—no swing; strike three. The ones who did hit were memorable and often received the offer letter.

As you talk with people, consider ways to lob the softball over the plate. Remove friction and set them up for success. Don't make it difficult for them to have a meaningful conversation.

The aha moment

I grew up in a small town in Kentucky. Every time I go back, I stop at my favorite breakfast place. It's a local spot—nothing fancy—but a great place for breakfast. You probably have a similar place in your hometown, or you have been to a place like that. This breakfast spot has homemade gravy, which is hard to find in a restaurant these days. If all you have ever had is instant gravy, you have not really had gravy. I grew up eating my mom's awesome biscuits and gravy. I think I could eat my body weight in biscuits and gravy.

So I'm sitting there, having biscuits and gravy, country ham, and coffee at breakfast with my sister. She said something profound, something that gave me such clarity I never forgot it: "You can't have someone else's aha moment for them. They have to have it for themselves." She said it in passing, without giving it much thought . . . and that's often where the great stuff comes from.

Think about it. You give someone good advice—the perfect solution to their problem. It will save them time and effort, and you expect them to be so thankful. But they aren't. How do we learn our best and most enduring lessons? What lessons stick with us for years? Those lessons we learn the hard way. Some things we learn from others; however, many of the lessons that stay with us are seared by pain and heartache into our memory banks. They endure. They stay with us because they cost us something.

You can't have someone else's aha moment for them.
They have to have it for themselves.

When you try to have someone else's aha moment for them, it doesn't cost them anything; therefore, it doesn't truly register as important. It should, but it doesn't. It just doesn't stick. If you have kids, or have spent time around kids, you already know this. They don't listen to your sage advice. Most of the time, they must experience their own pain before it sinks in. This is why we, as humans, keep making the same mistakes; it sounds great to learn from someone else's errors, but it doesn't always work that way.

My friend's son opened a checking account while he mowed lawns in high school. It came with a debit card and overdraft protection. His father advised caution, emphasizing how expensive the overdrafts were; the son didn't listen.

The father told me, "The day I stopped giving him advice was when he said, 'You know, Dad, some things in life are best learned through experience.' I wholeheartedly agreed and resolved not to mention it again. Guess what? The next day, the overdraft letters started pouring in—fifteen in all. It was an expensive lesson for him."

You can't have their aha moment for them. Don't curtail this process. Be patient and wait for it as they walk their own path. It's necessary and valuable.

Be gracious

When I hear you say, "If you remember, last time we were together, we talked about . . .," you're losing the war. Those words tell me, from your viewpoint, that I'm an idiot because I don't remember our last conversation. You're leveraging that to feel superior, because you remembered and I didn't. That's how it feels on this side of the conversation. If you need to refer to a previous conversation, that's fine, but don't do it like that. Calling me an idiot, whether out loud or between the lines, will put space between us. It won't help.

You may say it to make a point, but don't think it'll bring us closer together. I probably won't have a moment of self-reflection where I say aloud or to myself, "Oh, you're right—I'm an idiot. Thank you for pointing that out." Not going to happen. Again, it creates space between us; that's not my goal.

You certainly can remind someone of a previous conversation if you need to, but be intentional about your goal and choose your words carefully.

You can also be gracious by helping them remember. Sometimes in conversation, the other person forgets what they were about to say. It's as if the thought just fell out of their head. Help them out—remind them of what you were just talking about to prompt their memory, and wait there with them while they think. This shows you are on their side of the table. It's an important way to connect.

Cussing

In many circles, cursing is considered unprofessional. Where I grew up in Kentucky, we called it cussing. I personally struggle with this, as I grew up cussing like a sailor and I'm trying to stop. It's hard to unlearn some things that seem so ingrained. That cuss word and its accompanying feeling are lurking just below the surface, waiting for a chance to get out when my guard is down. Sometimes, it seems that the only right word is a cuss word—but do your best to resist.

It's an interesting phenomenon. Some people will rank curse words, considering one more offensive than another. Dropping a "Level 2" f-bomb might not work, but a milder "Level 1" four-letter word might be acceptable. You get the idea. Others are fine with any word you want to use. My point is, you don't know what's acceptable and what isn't. In my opinion, it's best to stay away from it altogether. Maybe I'm old school. You can make your own call on that one; it's something to consider.

One friend told me, "Cussing is cathartic." Another described it as a "release." Why is that? I don't know, but I believe it. Sometimes the emotion we feel desperately wants to come out as a bad word. But as my mother used to say, "That don't make it right."

A great illustration of this comes from a toddler. My wife was with a three-year-old, having a discussion about potty words. For clarity's sake, potty words from a three-year-old are words like *butt* or *stupid*. The toddler said he was not going to say potty words because he wasn't supposed to. Later that morning, she heard him use a few potty words. She asked, "I thought you said you were not going to use potty words?" He said, "I know I said I wasn't gonna say 'em, but I'm going to say 'em anyway." He wasn't being rebellious or disrespectful; he just wanted to say them. There's something about it you can't put your finger on.

Try not to curse. If you must, stay away from Level 2 cuss words.

The hard part is stopping cursing once you start. It seems as if they're connected—maybe with a string or something. Once you say one cuss word, it drags another out with it. They follow, rapid fire. It's easier not to turn the faucet on than to stop it midstream.

I mentioned that I grew up cussing like a sailor. Honestly, I'm not sure I've ever truly known a *real* sailor, but I hear they cuss a lot, so I'm going with it. There does seem to be some historical support for it, though. "It is an unfortunate fact that the sailor has a great tendency, unless it's checked, to become an artist in the use of profanity. He shares the tendency with most men under naval or military control . . . As a rule, he means nothing by it, and the habit grows so strong with him that it becomes second nature, or part of his language. But the unbridled use of profanity lowers the respect in which a man is held by his shipmates."[10]

All this said, it's tricky. I recommend you stay away from cursing altogether. I know what some will say: it's just part of who I am. To which I would say, remember, this isn't about you. Making the connection is about the other person. You want to meet them where they are—not make them come to you.

---

[10] *Naval Leadership*, 1939.

THE DYNAMIC DUO: REFLECTION AND INQUIRY

This one is so simple, yet it's pure gold. If you take nothing else from this book, walk away with these two words: *reflection* and *inquiry*. I've found them to be the most helpful two words I could give anyone looking to have a meaningful conversation. If you keep them at the forefront, it will transform your ability to connect with people.

STEP 1: REFLECTION

The first step in the Dynamic Duo is reflection. It's as simple as reflecting their content back to them. You're already listening intently, so it's easy to repeat what they said. It's like they're looking in a mirror, and you're speaking their words back to them. They could be telling a story, and they get to the good part: "Then the car in front of us just stopped in the middle of the road!"

Here's where you jump in *reflection.*

"What? No way! So you're doing 60 miles per hour, and the car in front of you just stopped?! In the middle of the road? Wow!"

This does good things for you.

It lets them know that you're right there in the car with them. They're driving and you're riding shotgun. You're following this story, and you want them to know that.

It helps with clarity and understanding. They have a chance to jump in and correct you or confirm and add to the details. You'll say things like:

- Let me be sure I understand you. What I hear you say is . . .
- So you're saying . . .
- You said . . .
- You're telling me that . . .
- Sounds like you're saying . . .

Words like these convey the idea of suspended judgment. In other words, "This is what I think you said, and I want you to tell me if I heard you correctly."

You can also reference earlier comments they made; it's another way to let them know you were listening to what they said and you remember it.

STEP 2: INQUIRY

After reflection, move into Step 2 of the Dynamic Duo, *inquiry*. Here's where you ask open-ended questions to dig deeper into what they said. Inquiry is like a shovel to dig in and uncover more details.

- "Wow! Sixty miles per hour to zero! Probably left some tire marks on the road. What happened next?"
- You might be after clarity. "Is this when you were driving the rental car?"
- Maybe there's a detail you're curious about. "You said it was raining. Was there standing water on the road? I'm thinking of hydroplaning right now."
- If they mention the antilock brakes kicking in when they jammed the brake pedal to the floor, you could ask, "Antilock brake cycling, I don't think I've ever been through that. What does that feel like?"

If there was something you didn't understand about the words they used, now is the time to ask. You might be at work and hear the word *accountability*. It's a big word that means so many different things to different people. That could look like any of these statements:

- "Accountability. That's a big word that can have lots of different meanings. Tell me how you would define it."
- "Walk me through how your team would see this."
- "Can you give me an example of accountability might look like?"
- "That sounds interesting. Tell me more about that."

Inquiry gives them an opportunity to talk more and further explain their thoughts and feelings around the topic. Remember, you're curious, so your goal is to keep the story going to find out more. You're also extending the conversation on their side of the table.

Never assume you know what they mean when they say something; always ask.

This does several things that encourage connection. They get to talk more. They get to explain their thoughts and feelings. You get to listen more and learn more. Remember, it's always about the other and rarely about you. When you can set self aside, you'll truly be on the path to great connection. Almost everyone is thinking, "I don't want to talk about you, I want to talk about me." They're all Toby Keith fans. When you focus on them, you become rare and memorable.

Let's look at another example of inquiry in action. Maybe they've just told you they're a professional skateboarder. To be honest, I don't need to know anything about the topic they bring up. I know nothing about professional skateboarders, nuclear physics, or how a news show puts on a broadcast. But with inquiry, I don't need to. I get to dig a little deeper and ask you to tell me about it.

The conversation might go something like this. "Did I hear you say you're a professional skateboarder? Really! That's so interesting. I've never met a professional skateboarder."

Any of these questions would play well as a next step:

- "Where would you go to compete? I would think SoCal."
- "How often do you get to compete?"
- "Do you make your own skateboard, or is it a custom rig you have special made?"
- "What about sponsorships? Do you have those stickers on your helmet when you skate? How do you get connected with companies like that?"
- "The only person I know in that business is Tony Hawk, one of the OGs. Have you ever met him?"

Obviously, I'm not peppering them with all these questions at the same time, but they're sprinkled into the conversation as appropriate.

There are layers of questions, starting with surface, factual queries that don't really get to the heart and emotion of a person. If it were a more personal setting, I would take it to the next level. I might dig in with questions like "How much travel do you have to do for that? Is that hard on your family?" "Is this a side hustle or your primary gig?" "Do you ever do these activities with your son?"

The setting will drive the questions you get to ask. Is it a dinner party, or is it a meal with a friend you haven't seen in a while?

If you tell me you're married, I could ask these questions:

- "You told me you're married. What's your wife's name, and how did y'all meet?"
- "You mentioned a son. How old is he, and what's he into at right now?"
- "You talked about a recent promotion. Has that caused you to have to work more hours? How are you and your family handling that?"

Great questions are windows into a person, allowing you to see them clearly. Ask them deep, probing questions, and see where it goes.

STORYTELLING

Skirts and stories

We all have a friend that takes five minutes to tell a two-minute story. Most everyone can hang on to a story for a couple of minutes; beyond that, unless it's a spectacular tale, distraction is likely. I personally will need to hear about blood or somebody getting arrested for it to go longer than two minutes.

Think of the point you're trying to make, and trim the story to include the details you need. Leave out the parts that don't help you land the point. Spending too much time on details takes away from the effectiveness of the story. It seems to drag on, and everyone will wonder when you're going to get to the point. Consider your story's impact. Think of it like a laser beam, precisely focused on the point you want to land.

A good speech should be like a woman's skirt;
long enough to cover the subject and short enough to
create interest.
—*Winston S. Churchill*

Don't slow down if you forget a detail

Sometimes we forget the details of a story as we're telling it. That's okay, but let it be a speed bump in the story, not a stop sign. If you forget part of a story, keep moving unless it's *absolutely* crucial. You'll lose momentum (and your audience) quickly when you stop midstory to recall an unimportant detail. Stopping midstream breaks the arc of the story. Once broken, it's hard to get back on track.

The Words You Use

If you can't remember an insignificant detail of a story, keep moving.

It might help to share an example. You and your friend have just ordered at Waffle House when he comes out with this: "Bill and I were having breakfast here the other day. Did you know he lost his job?"

You come back with the Dynamic Duo and say, "What! Lost his job? I haven't heard that. What happened?"

"Yeah, he got fired! He was telling me about what happened when our food showed up. I got the ham and cheese omelet . . . no, wait . . . was it a western? I remember it had cheese in it, and it was really good . . . but it escapes me what else was in it . . . hmm . . . and the server spilled coffee on the table too. All over my bullet journal. I was not happy . . . I'm thinking it was a western. Dang. Let me think for a second." And a long pause follows.

Here I am, in a holding pattern on the edge of my seat, wondering how my friend got fired. The story has gone off the rails and I'm asking myself, "Where are we going with this?" The momentum is lost, and I'm in limbo waiting for an unimportant detail that has no impact on the storyline. At this point, I'm no longer as interested as I was when the story began. Chasing that squirrel has derailed the arc.

Few things are as frustrating as this. You notice how it drains the momentum and excitement from the story. Bottom line: Don't do this to someone else.

Silence might be the best move

What about the words you don't use, the things you don't say? If someone is writing something down, I try to be quiet while they write it. Don't confuse them while they're writing. Don't add cognitive load. They can't process both things at the same time, so let them write. It gives them room to maneuver. If they thought it was important enough to write down, let them.

If you're asking yourself, "Should I speak now? Should I say this?," here's a great litmus test, a three-point question widely attributed to Craig Ferguson:

- Does this need to be said?
- Does this need to be said, right now?
- Does this need to be said, right now, by me?

If you answer yes to all three questions, then say it. However, if any of your answers are no, keep your mouth shut. It may *feel* good to say it, but it won't *do* any good. You might feel better afterward, but you might also alienate the other person in the process.

WHAT DOESN'T WORK

Don't skip the small talk

Some people are direct communicators who use few words. However, not everyone is wired that way. For others, small talk is the lubricant for social engagement. I understand that you may not be built for small talk, but remember: it's not about you—it's about them.

During a workshop, someone described how he interacts with his coworkers. As soon as they begin talking about an issue, he interrupts them with, "Do you want me to just listen, or do you want me to provide solutions? Because that'll frame how I respond to you." I've heard many people make a similar comment.

Yes, it gets right to the point, but it's transactional. There's little emotion in this approach.

First, I *always* want you to listen—so the answer to that part is yes. Second, I stay away from providing solutions. It works better when you draw out *their* solutions. Their ideas are always better than yours (or mine) because people always favor their own ideas over someone else's.

I'll listen and then say, "Man, that sounds tough. What are you going to do?" Or "Wow, that sounds crazy. What do you think your next step is?"

Hesitate to give advice

I'm so slow to give advice these days. I aggressively avoid it, and I'll use every technique in this book to get out of it. If you do get it out of me, it'll be painful for both of us. Okay, maybe I'm exaggerating, but you get the point. Make them work for it. They have to earn it. If they ask for advice, I dodge the question by asking a deeper question.

It's hard, though, because we're wired to give advice, whether solicited or not. We think we're saving them time and resources. We want to get them to their destination faster. In theory, that's how it works, but that's not the real world. Most of the time your advice doesn't sink in. It's just not fully heard. Even when someone asks for advice—even when they think they want it—what they really need most is to talk about it. If you wait them out, you'll see they'll be just fine without it.

It should be obvious, but I'll say it anyway: if they haven't even asked for advice, it probably won't be well received. Sometimes folks start a sentence with something along the lines of "Well, I'll tell you what you need to do . . ." Bless their heart. They jumped in with both feet but had no idea there were gators in the pool. It's not going to go well.

Keep your ideas, thoughts, and opinions to yourself as much as you can. Even if they ask. Advice is too easy to give when the pain is not your own.

Stay away from giving advice unless it's dragged out of you by a team of mules.

Another thing: my advice is my idea, not yours. There's far less buy-in when it's my idea. A coworker put a mental image in my head that has stuck with me for years: When you give them the solution in one hand, you give them the excuse for when it doesn't work in the other. When my suggestion falls flat on its face, they get to say, "Well, it was Keith's idea, and I didn't think it would work. Sure enough, it didn't." They have an easy out. They get to blame it on me, because it was my idea and not theirs. There's no emotional investment. When you give them the solution, you own the outcome.

> *When you give them the solution in one hand, you give them the excuse for when it doesn't work in the other.*

It's different when *they* come up with the idea—they're emotionally invested in its success. They're going to do everything they can to make it succeed. If it doesn't, it looks bad on them (versus me).

It sounds like such a tame question: "What would you do?" Watch out. It's a trap, a vortex, too easy to get sucked in. Don't get caught in that gravitational pull.

One way to dodge the advice question is to ask what solutions they've thought up or already tried. Ask them what other ideas they might have. Ask them enough questions, and they'll come to some good conclusions on their own, which is exactly what you want.

IF YOU MUST GIVE ADVICE . . .

If you *do* give advice (Did I mention not to give advice?), remember that your advice becomes their choice. No matter how good your advice is, they can choose not to follow it. Give advice only when you must, then let it go. Don't get upset if they don't heed it. You can't want it more than them. Don't become emotionally invested. Disconnect yourself from the effort and the outcome.

> *Your advice becomes their choice. They can choose not to follow it.*

If you must give advice, wait for the right time. Wait for them to ask. If you give it before then, you're casting pearls before swine. It won't be appreciated, it won't be received, and it may even make them angry or upset. Wait for it.

If you're going to give some tough advice to someone, it's best to prep the battlespace. Ask for permission first. "Can I say something that might be kind of hard right now?" This opens their mind for that hard thing you feel like you have to say. It's a game changer when someone gives you permission, and it's rare for them to say no.

Another way to prep the battlespace is to make them ask two or three times—that way I know they really want it. I'll draw out their ideas with questions, then set them up to receive it well. "I'm not sure my idea would work; are you sure you want to hear it?" Their yes opens the door to their mind. They're more likely to receive your advice when you get their agreement beforehand, when they open the door for you. When you make them draw the advice out of you, it becomes solicited. They really, really want it. You've made them work so hard to get it they'll hang on to every word.

You May Win the Battle, but You'll Lose the War

On a related note: If I force my opinion on you when the stakes are low, if I pummel you into agreement over an unimportant detail, the quality of our connection will suffer. I may have been right, but it came at a cost. That's what I call winning the battle but losing the war.

If my wife is telling a story about how we almost had an accident with a blue car, and I jump in and correct her with, "It was really a red car," is that going to help anything? No. Does it impact the story? No. Am I going to win the battle but lose the war? Yes.

In other words, I've scored a short-term tactical victory (I was right) that resulted in a long-term strategic loss (I sounded petty, and that put distance between us). You must play the long game if you want great connections.

No one likes to be talked over

When someone talks over you, you should stop talking. It's intentional. They heard you talking just like you heard them, but they intentionally chose to continue to talk over *your* talking. When that happens, I typically don't repeat what I said unless they ask. If they don't ask me to repeat it, they wouldn't have listened anyway. At least I know that if they ask, they'll be quiet enough to listen when I repeat myself.

I've been talked over, and it makes me want to say it again, louder, to make sure I'm heard. However, if they didn't listen the first time, they probably won't hear it the second time, either. Let it go. Move on to the next part of the conversation. If they really want to know, they'll ask you to say it again.

Horn honking

At the end of the road I live on is an intersection on a busy main thoroughfare. There's no turn lane at the light, so it can be a bit challenging sometimes. The other day a person turned across traffic right in front of me! I laid on my horn; I had to put the brakes on to keep from T-boning them.

What were they thinking? I had the right of way!

As I'm driving away from the intersection, I asked myself, Should I have honked at that person? Well, maybe so. Maybe they deserved it. But will it change their behavior? Will they start waiting for the other person instead of turning in front of them, forcing them to put their brakes on? We think honking at someone as they run the red light or turn left in front of us will make them stop running red lights and turning left in front of people.

My conclusion—and I bet it matches yours—is that no, it likely won't change their behavior. We've all heard that honk, and yet we still run red lights and turn in front of people. And when we see others do it, we still honk at *them*. *They* need to change, right? I think we all know laying on the horn won't make any difference; it only makes us feel better.

Honking is like telling someone the truth without love. A honk doesn't show love. You wouldn't pull up to your date's house and honk for her to come out, right? That generally doesn't work well with her father. Truth without love just doesn't work. No one will listen.

Maybe you say it, and maybe it's right. But if it's said without love and compassion, it probably won't be received. If it's not received, what good did it do to say it?
—*Nick Person*

The point is, don't say something just to make yourself feel better. We've all said these things, but they don't help. They don't encourage conversation. Things like that put a mile between you and them. Once you get that far apart, it's hard to recover. We say these things, hoping they'll realize their errant position. But just because you turn the mirror around and show someone who they really are doesn't mean they want to see it. When we speak in judgment, our words are harsh and often fall on deaf ears. They also fall on hurt feelings.

Too many words

There should be a warning signal that goes off in your head when you've heard yourself talking for a long time. If you find yourself in that place, when you hear that signal going off, just stop midsentence.

If you find yourself talking too much, just stop.

Say something like, "You know, I've been talking way too much here. Too many words. What are your thoughts right now?" Or end your sentence quickly and transition into a question to get the other person talking. Chances are they've been waiting for a chance to jump in.

Don't fill the space with more words.
Say less with more effect.

Everything sounds like a question

I talk with some people who have a raised inflection in their voice at the end of their sentences. This can make every sentence sound like a question, and I'm not sure if they're asking me something or just talking. Try to avoid this, as it can be challenging in conversation.

Don't be the *no* guy

Instead of trying to explain this one, I'll illustrate it with a story. My wife and I stayed at a vacation rental cottage, a small one-bedroom farmhouse in the middle of a hayfield. It was a wonderful experience.

We were sitting on the front porch swing, talking. She said, "I would love to have a small place like this and rent it out." She makes sourdough bread, and she added that she would leave a small loaf of sourdough bread for each visitor.

I thought to myself, What a great idea! Then, right after that wonderful thought, the next thought came in: What if something goes wrong with the bake, and someone gets sick? This great idea might expose us to lawsuits and liability. My wife is the dreamer; I tend to be a bit more pragmatic, to my detriment.

I almost opened my mouth and said these things, but I paused. I loved the farmhouse idea, and if money were no object, we would build it. But money is always an object. The reality is, we will likely never build a small farmhouse like that and start our own rental business. If that's the case, why destroy the dream? If the dream brings happiness, let it be. Don't be the *no* guy and destroy the dream.

When you're the *no* guy, you're the dream crusher. You're Negative Nelly.

(I'm so sorry for that if your name is Nelly.)

You're the one who stands between a wonderful possibility that *could* be and the cold hard world that *is*. Nobody likes that guy.

> *Don't be the no guy.*

Instead, my answer should be something simple. "That's a great idea! I love that. Your bread is so good! I know that would make it special." Let the dream live. If you never build that small farmhouse, it's not your fault. But when you're the *no* guy, it *is* your fault, even when it isn't. You get the blame for stating the obvious. My recommendation: don't be that guy.

Jumping in with a better story

Have you ever been in a relationship where someone always had a bigger, better story? While talking with an acquaintance, we realized we shared a mutual friend, Dan. Dan was a military aviator for many years. They would go on an annual camping trip with a bunch of other guys. He laughingly said, "Anytime we were sitting around the campfire telling stories, we learned to let Dan go last because he told the most incredible stories. No one could top him! He would always start his stories out with, 'There I was, flying along at six hundred miles per hour, three hundred feet above the ground. You'll never guess what happened next!'"

Don't get me wrong: Dan told some incredible stories and had a fascinating past. But when you leverage that too often, it can wear thin after a while. Even though he made his comment lightheartedly, I could hear the underlying edge to it.

We've all got great stories. As a military guy, I've got dozens of crazy stories that are too incredible to make up, but I don't tell them too often. I don't want to be that guy. Sometimes it's better to let others be in the limelight.

Another attribute of storytelling is to never be the hero of your own story. It can come across as self-serving, as if you have it all together. It gets old fast.

> *Never be the hero of your own story.*

I know you want to tell the story of the time when you got it perfectly right despite all the odds stacked against you! Don't we all. There's a little bit of a braggadocio in all of us. But you must keep those stories to yourself. The times when you can tell them are rare—usually only to your spouse, your mom, or maybe your best friend.

STOP WITH THE CORNY JOKES

I used to be an electric meter reader back in the day. I walked from house to house to read the meter to determine the electric usage. I can't tell you how many times I would walk through the yard to read the meter, and the homeowner would say, "You can just skip it; we didn't use any electricity this month." Then they would laugh hysterically, as if they were at a nightclub watching some famous stand-up comic. I would force a smile and a laugh and keep moving. It was funny the first time, but after a few dozen times of hearing that one, not so much.

Corny jokes don't play. Stay away from them; people have already heard them all. Even if they haven't, they're tired and overused. There are so many other, better ways to begin a conversation. These things create walls and barriers to communication and connection. You may be tempted to make a lame joke, but don't.

To sum it all up, be intentional about the words you use. Most of us throw them around without a lot of thought, but I would encourage you to think them through before you throw them out there.

CHAPTER 7

The Genius Is in the Question

Judge a man by his questions rather than by his answers.
—Voltaire

A FEW YEARS AGO, I was exposed to a powerful yet simple problem-solving methodology called the Delta Technique. I won't go into all the details, but a key part of its success is in asking questions: what we know, what we don't know, and what we need to know, to name a few. The goal was to ask great questions to establish a common knowledge base for everyone. These questions also helped to clearly define the problem.

One part of the Delta Technique that caught me off-guard was the amount of time spent in identifying and defining the problem before trying to solve the problem. Most of the time, we jump right into problem-solving mode before we fully understand what's going on. Knowing everything we can know about the problem helps us solve it. This is what makes a great question so powerful.

Asking great questions is the key to the kingdom.

Of course, the other side of this is analysis paralysis. Spending too much time admiring the problem isn't healthy, but I do think the sweet spot is somewhere between the two. There's magic in asking the right question. When you ask the right question at the right time, you may be the only one asking questions. That's when you become rare and memorable.

The genius is in the question.
—Buddy Hobart

The easier option is to provide answers. We're all smart, but sometimes we're wrong. Other times, we're at the end of our suggestion rope and don't have anything left. The genius is in the question, not the answer. The harder thing is to listen, and I mean really listen, so you can ask great questions.

Take notes

We've talked a little about taking notes during conversation. Ask clarifying questions, and take notes as you go. These things help you connect the dots. For example, if someone tells you that they got married in March, and then a few minutes later they mention that they met that special someone in January, jump into the conversation and ask about that. In that example, they weren't engaged very long; there's got to be more to the story. Go ahead, ask them about it! It opens the door to a deeper conversation. "Wow! That's a quick engagement. Tell me about how you went from meeting to married in just a few months."

When I ask what makes someone good at conversation, a frequent response is that they ask questions about what was said. One person responded with deep emotion in their voice, "When I come across someone that's good at follow-up questions—wow."

Think of a time when someone was telling you a story, maybe about the time they had a flat tire. You might think, "I'll tell the story of when I had a flat tire, and that'll be a shared experience we have together. This shared experience will draw us closer."

That's an okay move. It might work. But here's the thing: they wanted to tell their story without competition. My suggestion? Don't steal their thunder. When you tell a similar story, you've just taken their unique experience and made it common. It's not special anymore because someone else has had the same experience.

You've seen social media posts where a person talks about their trip to the Rocky Mountains, and someone else jumps in to talk about how great their trip to the Rockies was. They just hijacked the post. If we're not careful, telling our story can be like hijacking a post. It lets the air out of their tires.

Don't take their unique experience and make it commonplace.

Here's a better move: ask them to tell the story of how they changed the flat tire. Keep the focus on them. You might have an incredible story about the time you got a flat and Arnold Schwarzenegger stopped to help you change it. Yes, the Terminator, the Governator! But now is not the time to tell that story. Now is the time to focus on them.

Review your notes

I'll continue to emphasize this: while you're talking with someone, take notes about the key topics. You can't remember everything, so write a few things down. Let them see you taking notes. You might even say something like, "Man, that's good. I gotta write that down." Then, before your next conversation, look back over your notes from your last conversation so you can bring it up. "Last time we talked, you mentioned _____. How has that been going lately?" Asking great questions connected to your last conversation shows that you cared enough to remember and revisit the key points.

When you remember the names of their family, a vacation they were planning on taking, or a particular challenge they were facing at work, you demonstrate your investment in them. Trust me; they'll notice. Most people don't remember the details. They don't forget on purpose, they just don't purposefully remember.

When you're intentional, you stand out.

Most people aren't forgetful on purpose; they just don't purposefully remember.

Even if you tell them that you took notes last time and looked over your notes before this conversation, it still has impact. You thought enough of them last time you were together to write down the important things, then look at it before you got together again. People notice. They remember.

After these conversations, spend some time looking over your notes. Some of it probably looks like chicken scratch: half sentences, abbreviations, or maybe even just a word or two. Go back while it's still fresh and add context. Flesh things out. Add anything you missed. Include explanatory notes and information. Clarify your shorthand. Rewrite it so you can read it. If you wait too long, you'll forget the gist of the conversation, and half of it won't mean anything to you. In the moment, you thought it was important enough to write down; follow it up with intentionality and polish.

THE ART OF THE FOLLOW-UP QUESTION

The follow-up is one you ask that is directly related to what someone just said. It lets them know you heard them. It shows them you're curious about what they're talking about, and you want to know more. They think, Wow, someone is interested in me. That's rare in our busy world. And it's powerful.

The follow-up question is so easy. Dig deeper into their comment. It's like a conversational shovel. Here's what it might look like:

- "Tell me more about that." (This is a wonderful question to ask. I only have one question on a sticky note on my computer—and this is the one!)

- "Tell me a story about that feeling you just mentioned."
- "What was that like?"
- "How did that feel?"
- "Expand on that for me."
- "That's a big word you just used that can mean a lot of things. Walk me through what you're thinking."
- "What does that look like in your world?"
- "Give me an example of how that plays out."
- "Put that in context for me. When you say _____, what do you mean by that?"
- "I'm not sure I'm following you. Can you say that a different way?"

It can be as simple as "You said you're a muscle car fanatic. What's your favorite muscle car? If money were no object, which one would you buy?" And then followed with, "What is it about the '68 Camaro that makes it the One?" It's a specific question laser focused on what they just said. That's a softball lobbed over the plate, right in the strike zone. I do it on purpose because I want them to knock it out of the park.

Seek clarity

Sometimes you're not sure what they're talking about. Maybe they've rambled a bit in their conversation and you're having trouble keeping up with where they're going. Don't assume you completely understand them, because you may be way off base. Use the follow-up question to gain clarity. "I hear the angst in your voice as you talked about your weekend visit with your in-laws, but I not sure I'm following all that. Walk me through that again." It shows interest, curiosity, and a desire to fully understand. I'm letting you drive, and I'm riding shotgun.

Motivation is a great topic to ask about. Any time you can ask about thoughts and feelings, you're starting to get in the deep end of the pool. Better connections happen in the deep water.

Don't just agree with someone for the sake of being agreeable. Ask them a probing question about it, with an open vibe of suspended judgment. "I've always looked at climate change like X; I've never looked at it like Y. Not sure I'm there yet, but keep talking. Tell me more."

Following up later

If someone mentions an important thing in a conversation, be intentional to follow up on it afterward. This is especially important if you've asked about it.

Let's say that your friend lost their job a few months ago. During our conversation, they mention a job interview coming up later this week, on Thursday. When Friday rolls around, reach out to your friend to ask how the interview went.

Or maybe a friend told you they're going on vacation next month. That's an important topic that I would want to follow up on after they get back.

But the follow-up is also easy to forget. Life is busy for everyone, so let's use our systems to enable success. A great way to remember the follow-up is to put it on your calendar. When your friend talks about their vacation next month, they mention that they're coming home on the fifteenth. I'll create a calendar event on the seventeenth labeled "Check in with Tom," and in the comments I'll mention where they went on vacation and how long they were gone. It's a small gesture, but it's one most people fail to do. Little things like that demonstrate that you care enough to remember and ask about it.

Not asking questions can make you appear uninterested

As a senior military officer, I would often visit teams and divisions in their workspace. During those visits, they would talk about their mission and some of the challenges they faced. For too many of those visits, I didn't ask questions. I knew they had worked hard to prepare, and I didn't want to put them on the spot with a question they didn't know the answer to. I listened politely but didn't go any further.

It sounded great to me, but what did it look like to them? It probably seemed disengaged and uninterested. If I didn't ask a single question, how did they know I even listened to what they said? Did I really hear them? Did I even care? They've invested all this time to be ready for me, and they walked away from it thinking that I wasn't interested. However unintentional it was, the message was still the same.

The moral of the story: When you're listening to someone and you don't ask any questions, it can come across as disengaged and uninterested. That's generally the last thing you want to convey. So be curious and ask a few good questions. You'll find out some interesting things when you do.

Ask deep questions

If you want to get in the deep end of the pool, ask deep questions. These touch emotional places and trigger greater connection. Not every situation requires a deep question. Standing in line at the grocery with a stranger might not be the time. But when the time is right, it can help create connection.

Deep questions go below the surface. They involve

- Feelings
- Motivations
- Emotions
- Goals and dreams
- Aspirations

Bucket list questions are an easy place to start if you have no idea what to say. Some examples:

- "Tell me something on your bucket list that you've recently done."
- "Is there anything on your bucket list that's coming up soon?"

Other examples might also include:

- "Tell me what keeps you at your current employer?"
- "How are your aging parents doing these days?"

Deep questions are key ways to connect. They touch places inside of us that often don't get an opportunity to see the light of day.

DEFINE THE BIG WORDS

When you hear a big word, ask them to define it. So many words mean so many different things to people. One good example of this might be the word *inclusion*. That word means a lot of things, depending on who's defining it. To better engage, simply ask what it means.

It could look like this: "You've mentioned the word *inclusion*. That word means different things to different people. Walk me through how you define inclusion, and give me an example of what that might look like to you." That gives them a chance to be seen and heard, which is what most people want. It also brings clarity to the discussion and helps you with more follow-up questions.

ASK SOMETHING IN THEIR WHEELHOUSE

If you want to have a good conversation, ask someone about their field of expertise. If they're an expert in ancient Mayan culture, ask them about it. Maybe it's not a field you're terribly interested in. But there's always room to learn something new. Ask them to tell you two or three interesting things they discovered about Mayan culture. Ask what they think led to the decline of that civilization. You'll be surprised at how quickly a fascinating conversation can develop.

People love to talk about things they're passionate about. They've invested significant time and energy into a topic, so ask them about it. It's like hitting oil in the Alaskan wilderness.

DON'T ASK IF YOU DON'T CARE

Ask a great question, then sit back to really listen. If you're not that interested in the answer, then don't ask the question. People can usually tell when you're not listening. If you ask me a question and then ignore my answer, I'm wondering why you asked in the first place. It's better not ask than to ask and not listen.

ABC: Always be curious.
—Luis Rivera

In summary, remain curious. Never have a know-it-all mentality. Always assume that there's more to know, more you can learn from someone.

Remember, everyone has answers. What you really need is great questions.

CHAPTER 8

Emotions

The most important thing in communication is hearing what isn't said.
—Peter Drucker

I was having a Java Summit with a friend I've known for many years. He said something so powerful that, when he said it, I wrote it down straightaway:

The heart connects people.

Absolutely. We can feel it when we're talking with someone. It's like lightning in a bottle.

The heart connects people. We don't get enough of that in our modern world. It's so obvious and so much more than transactional.

The heart connects us because emotions often override reason, and their pull is far stronger than logic. That's why they say love is blind. We fall for someone even when our brain says, "Bad idea."

Let's acknowledge that emotions are strong and hard to overcome. When emotion is involved, it's hard to change direction. It's like trying to turn the Titanic with a dinner plate for a rudder—it just ain't gonna happen. With the strength of our emotions in mind, let's explore how we can wrestle a bit of control from them and leverage the strength of our emotions to create connection.

Look for the Tattoo

The tattoo is low-hanging fruit. It's one of the easiest ways to connect with someone. When you see a tattoo, ask them to tell the story of how they got it. I've never met anyone who wasn't excited to talk about their tattoo. I've also never met someone who had a boring story about their tattoo, and there's often a lot of emotional energy connected to it. Nobody ever says, "I just went and got a tattoo, end of story." There's always a backstory, there's always emotion, and they love to tell that story. It's something in their life they're proud of—a milestone, a significant event. Explore that. Give them an opportunity to tell their story, Johari window–style.

We Assign Motivation Where There Is None

Picture yourself in rush-hour traffic. We're on our way to a concert, and someone cuts us off. We get upset with them, maybe even angry. Not road-rage style, but frustrated. We're grumbling about them to ourselves.

In that discussion, we assign motivation to them. We know why they did this heinous and uncaring act . . .

. . . because we can read their mind, of course.

We come up with all kinds of reasons. They think they're better than us. They think their journey is more important than ours. But do we really know what's going on in their thoughts or their lives? They could be on the way to see a loved one in the hospital. They might be late for work. Perhaps they never even saw you. Or they forgot to look in the mirror before they changed lanes.

Don't assign motivation. Most of the time we're wrong. Remember the "suspend judgment" section? Let's revisit that thought. Don't cross the Bridge of Decision. It's not going to help you anyway.

Name Your Emotions

I was working with a group of leaders, and one of them began talking about critical conversations. He said, "In our organization, we've given it a name. We say, 'Let's have a critical conversation.' Critical conversations are hard enough already, so naming them makes them easier to have." There's wisdom right there.

When you put a name to a feeling, it makes it easier to say it, to get it out. It takes the edge off. I've heard it said, "When you name it, you can tame it." It helps you to grasp what's causing you so much angst. You can begin to move forward. Until you can do that, it's an unsettling unknown that will consume your mental energy.

> *When you can name your emotions,*
> *you can begin to control them.*
> *—Mike Pettinelli*

I often lead a workshop on delegation. It's a tough topic for leaders because all leaders struggle with it. I always ask why we don't delegate, and the answers are amazingly similar every time. It always boils down to trust, fear, and risk. These are the emotions below the reasons. Naming them is the first step in being able to understand them and control them.

We can feel this when we go to the doctor. Maybe I've got a pain in my side, and I'm worried that something is wrong with my kidney. I've done a cursory internet search, and now I'm sure I'm dying. We tend to catastrophize. But when I go to the doctor, he says, "It's just an obstruction in your kidney. We'll have to do a procedure and probably run a course of antibiotics, but you'll be fine." The diagnosis puts a name on it and gives me the ability to get a handle on my emotions. It's a significant issue, but now I can begin to deal with it.

My second time in prison

After graduating from officer training, my first assignment was at Mather AFB in Sacramento. I was a second lieutenant, finished with navigator training, and waiting for my next training course to begin. I was what they called a "casual" officer, assigned to whatever duty was needed.

One day, I was assigned to escort military prisoners to do a cleanup detail on base. They needed an officer to supervise them. I immediately had images of chain gangs and shotguns, but it turned out to be nothing like that. It was pretty tame—but getting there is the story.

I showed up at the jail and knocked on the front door. (Turns out you can't just walk into a jail; they have to let you in.) I told the guy that I was there to escort the prisoners on their work detail. He motioned to a chair in the lobby, and I sat to wait until they were ready to go. He told me they would be ready in about thirty minutes.

As I waited, I began to feel nervous, but I couldn't figure out why. If you knew me for any amount of time, you'd know that I'm not typically nervous. And knowing that just increased the nerves *because I'm never nervous*. I was jittery and couldn't figure out what's going on.

This went on for about ten minutes until I came to a realization: I noticed the smell of stale urine. Smell has always been the strongest sense memory trigger for me (and it turns out that science supports my intuition—of all our senses, smell has the strongest link to memory and emotion[11]).

That day in the lobby of the jail, I traveled back in time to the mock POW camp and my time in solitary confinement. I'd spent several hours alone in a dark and poorly ventilated cell with a coffee can in the corner for emptying my bladder. I left that training environment with powerful memories that were triggered by the smell of the jail that day.

Back at the jail, I realized what was going on. I was still nervous as a cat, but now I understood why. I was able to put a name on it. I sat there waiting for about fifteen more minutes, still nervous, but in control.

We eventually went to the commissary parking lot, where I watched the prisoners pick up trash. When they were all done, I helped escort them back to jail.

I was a little disappointed that I didn't even get a shotgun or a pair of mirrored sunglasses, *Cool Hand Luke* style. Actually, it was probably

---

[11] Hamer, 2019.

for the best they didn't give me a shotgun. If anyone had run away, I wouldn't have known what to do.

Fairly mundane overall, but I learned a lot about myself that day.

Trust is paramount

This really hit home for me one morning during a Java Summit with a dear friend. We were getting ready to get into the deep end of the pool. I could see it coming. He got this look on his face and hesitated for a moment—so I waited for it. He looked me right in the eye, very intentionally, with a little bit of a squint in his eye, and asked, "Can I trust you?"

Wow. Straight to the heavy stuff.

Some people don't ever open up. Maybe they're scared of what will happen when they start talking about it, or they don't have anyone they can trust that much. It could be that they want to remain very private. Maybe all these things were going through my friend's head as we were having coffee that morning. Now you understand the gravity of the situation, where we were. My friend began to tell the story of his marital challenges; much of it was of his own doing, which made it ever harder to talk about.

Once you're faced with the trust question, either directly or indirectly, you know something big is coming down the pike. Once it gets serious, you'd better get serious too. When you have someone's trust, they may choose to share a sacred reality with you. It's a rare gem to be appreciated when it's brought out into the light. Once our moment passes, it'll quickly be hidden again.

This gem holds a special place in their reality. Handle it with care, for not many people will get this invitation. If you minimize or trivialize their vulnerability, you'll damage the connection and close doors that are hard to reopen, if that's even possible.

Don't underestimate these times. To be fully known is so important, yet so rare. Sometimes I get the honor of being with people as they share from the heart. They get to be fully known. When you're friends with someone who is a safe place, someone you can completely trust, you cherish that friendship.

Treat these moments with reverence and respect, for in them you know you've been successful in being a true friend. This sharing of their deep feelings and emotions creates a strong connection. You know where their struggles are.

TRUST IS EASILY ERODED

Trust is added incrementally, in ounces, and taken away disproportionally, in pounds. It comes very slowly and is eroded very quickly. It's very fragile and hard to rebuild once broken. If they think you'll be talking about this conversation to anyone in the break room, they won't open up. We all know people who aren't good at keeping things to themselves, and we're careful what we say around them. I knew someone whose unofficial, behind-his-back nickname was "The Mouth of the South." Ouch. If you have a habit of telling secrets, then be up front about it. If someone says, "Please keep this to yourself," you should just jump in and say, "I'm terrible at secrets, so don't tell me."

Confidentiality is so important when we're talking about trust and deep-seated emotional things. It should go without saying that you should keep these things to yourself, but then again common sense isn't so common. If you're the Mouth of the South, folks aren't going to open up to you.

If you must talk about it, sanitize it first. As a military aviator, we would sanitize before a combat mission. We'd take our patches off and leave behind any identifying information. That way, if we were captured, they would have a hard time identifying who we were and what we were doing.

It works the same in conversations. If you're going to repeat the story, sanitize it. Remove any identifying details that could connect it to someone. If I'm telling a story from yesterday, I'll characterize it as happening "within the past few weeks." I even do my best not to identify the gender of the person I've been talking to unless it's important in the story. And I only tell the story if it will help them get to a better place.

Another example comes from my short four-month stint in IT. A co-worker was describing a software package he was developing as a side hustle. He asked me not to talk about it with our supervisor, because it was a product that they might want to take over and incorporate into our employer's product line. I agreed not to say anything. We continued our conversation, and he described his venture. A few weeks later, he said something about being able to trust me. When I asked what he meant, he said, "Do you remember that software I've been working on? I made that up. When a few weeks went by and you didn't tell our supervisor, I knew I could trust you." He was a believer in the advice of "Trust but verify."

SHOW SOME VULNERABILITY

Be appropriately vulnerable. When people ask me how things are going, my answer sounds something like this: "It's good. It ain't Facebook, it ain't perfect. I got issues I'm dealing with, but it's good." They probably don't want to hear everything I've got going on, but I don't want to give the impression that I've got it all together.

When you share your vulnerability, you point to your imperfectness. My sister said, "Once I hear that, I can say to myself: 'You're not perfect, either; we can be friends.'" No one likes to be around someone who acts like everything in their life is great. We all know that no one's life is perfect; we may put on a good face, but we've all got issues. If you pretend you don't, you're only fooling yourself. Acting like you have it all together appears inauthentic. You're a fake, a phony. No one trying for real connection wants those words said of them.

You also must be vulnerable to some extent before others will go there. Some folks will only go as far as *you* go. Model vulnerability, and you'll see it in others. These shared emotions lead to increased connections. When we've shared deeply with each other, a bond is developed.

Friendship is born at the moment when one person says to another: "What! You too? I thought I was the only one."
—C. S. Lewis

Friendship is hindered when we don't get real, when we don't share. I was talking with a friend who said, "Show me your humanity so that we can be friends." In other words, if you won't get real with me, if you won't show me the chinks in your armor, we won't be able to get close.

Politics and emotions

I once coached a leader who had very strong political opinions. My recommendation was to be careful and intentional. When you come out with these strongly held opinions, you'll alienate half the people you're speaking to. You have the right to believe whatever you want, but you also have to accept that others have that right also, to believe something different. If you want to connect, you must let them have their own opinions without vilifying them.

I know a guy on the other side of the aisle, and he's loud about it. It's everything he is, all the time. It would take great effort for me to set that aside to really connect, because of the volume of his opinion. It could be done, but it would come at a cost that I'm likely not willing to pay. When I spend energy just trying to get past that, I don't have much energy left for anything more.

As a result, I rarely entertain political topics; there's just too much emotion bottled up in those conversations. Realize that when you share your views, you're probably not going to change anything about the other person's opinions. Additionally, these conversations usually go south quickly. We rarely solve anything and generally get nowhere.

Your experience isn't the same

Don't ever start a sentence with "That exact thing happened to me one time. I was at a coffee shop . . ." What you went through isn't what they went through. It might be similar, but your journeys aren't the same. When you equate your experience to theirs, you minimize their reality. It's like saying "That's no big deal; I've been through that." You would never say that out loud, but that's what this sounds like. It just doesn't work. They'll listen politely but mentally dismiss you.

I know someone who lost a close friend who was in his twenties, with most of life's potential still in front of him. That's a significant emotional event. I can just hear the well-intentioned but tone-deaf responses. "Well, at least you still have other friends." Yes, but none of them can replace the one I've lost. "Yes, I know how you feel; last year we lost our dog, and it was so traumatic." For the record, I'm a dog person. However, losing a close family member, a child, or friend is different than losing a pet, no matter how beloved that pet was.

Recognize their experience first. If you get a chance later, you can tell your story, but the conversation may move on first. When they're telling their story, let that time be about them. Don't pull focus.

Listen in high gear

One of the questions I always ask during coaching sessions is this: "What's your biggest challenge right now?"

I was coaching a leader one morning and asked that question. Things got quiet for a few moments, and I could see the emotion on their face. It was clear they were getting ready to talk about something hard. They said, "This is something we haven't touched on yet." They took a deep breath, let it out, and paused again.

I knew we were about to get into the deep end of the pool.

During these moments, amp up your listening. It's okay to miss a few details if someone is talking about the football game over the weekend, but when things get personal, you can't zone out. If you have to ask them to repeat something more than once, you're not listening well enough.

Poor listening also diminishes their desire to share. The momentum in those deep discussions is so easily lost. I've been in places where I've begun to share personal things, but the other person's poor responses curtailed my desire to talk further. If you're not listening when I talk about something close to my heart, I don't want to continue. I'll just stop and move onto something in the shallow end.

Watch for the visible cues of the deep end, and then kick your listening skills into high gear.

GRIEF IS IN A LEAGUE OF ITS OWN

In fact, grief carries its own category. There are so many different forms of grief and trauma. Entire library wings could be written about what to say to someone who is grieving, and I'm no expert in that. One thing I do know, though, is to heed the advice from my hostage-negotiator friend: don't say, "I know how you feel." That assumes something you *can't* know. This advice harkens back to my hostage negotiator friend, but it bears repeating: Never forget that everyone's grief journey is different.

Sometimes just being there is key. Presence is often the beginning of what they need. You really don't have to say much; besides, there are no magic words. Time is an irreplaceable resource. We can't get any more of it, so when you spend it on someone during a tough time, it's noticed and appreciated. Your presence says "I care for you" more than routine conversation. The heart knows, and sometimes it'll tell you to be silent.

HISTORY AND EMOTIONAL BAGGAGE

Your history with the person affects the engagement. When you meet someone for the second time, you've got baggage from the previous encounter. Sometimes that's good, sometimes not. Either way, you'll bring all that to the next discussion with them.

If it wasn't a good experience, you'll probably have to work hard to overcome the baggage. We all know folks we dread talking to. If we're not careful, those emotions will come out during our interactions. Realizing this beforehand can help you deal with it.

At one point in my military career, I taught flight procedures to C-130 aircrews. In a crew airplane (as opposed to a single-seat airplane), the crew works for the pilot-in-command. We see this example in the airline industry; in this case, the flight attendants work for the captain in the cockpit.

Our history with someone impacts our ability to connect.

I once flew with a navigator student who was afraid to tell the pilot to turn the airplane. A big part of the navigator's job is to tell the pilot what heading to turn the airplane to, so this was a problem. This pilot was higher up in their organization and had authority over the navigator. The pilot also had an "I'm never wrong" personality. This navigator had baggage from previous negative engagements and was afraid of retribution after we landed. Even though his primary job was to navigate the airplane, he was afraid to. The baggage was real. So in this case, as the instructor, I had to intervene and tell the pilot to turn.

How to ditch the baggage

At one point in my career, I was working with a person I didn't particularly care for. It was not an active dislike, but we didn't get along very well for various reasons. However, we needed to get along for our organization to run smoothly. I asked someone I worked closely with to keep an eye on me to ensure I treated this person just like everyone else. This made an impact in multiple ways.

First, I spoke it out loud. There's great power in the spoken word—power to make things become a reality. If you speak it, it's more likely to come to pass in your own life. And when you speak it out loud, you also hear it. It lands in different place in your head, and it sinks in deeper.

Second, I made a commitment to a friend about where I wanted to be. It wasn't his idea; it was my idea. I owned the outcome. That's different than someone telling me that I need to get along with this person.

Third, I asked someone close to hold me accountable. In reality, 90 percent of the time, he would never see my interactions with this person. Then again, he might ask me about it the next time we saw each other, and I would have to tell him how it was going. Accountability is the high-octane gas that accelerates the engine. Let's leverage the discomfort of accountability to help us get where we want to be.

Feelings follow actions

We talked about this in the Mindshift chapter, but I want to revisit it here because it's so powerful.

Act first; feelings will follow.

This is counterintuitive. I want to *feel* like doing something before I do it, but it doesn't always work that way.

---

*We don't feel our way into action;
we act our way into feelings.*

I travel quite a bit for work. Often when I get to the hotel lobby, there's cookies right there at check-in. I essentially never *don't* want cookies. However, there are plenty of reasons why I might need to stay away from the cookies. Maybe it's about weight; maybe my blood sugar isn't great. Maybe I'm heading to supper in thirty minutes and don't want to ruin my appetite.

My head is telling me one thing (Don't eat the cookie.), and my heart is telling me another (You want the cookie, it's only one, eat the cookie!). Notice the period versus the exclamation point in those two opposing thoughts. Remember how much stronger our emotions are than our logical reasoning? That's the battle: the exclamation point versus the period.

If I always go with my feelings, I'm going to weigh three hundred pounds. I have to slow down and think. I have to act the way I know I should, not the way I feel—and my feelings will follow eventually.

Leverage the Gravitas

People say the most wonderful, powerful things. Sometimes I'm leading a workshop and someone says something amazing. Maybe it's an insight about themselves or a tough situation, or maybe it's just something cool. Whatever it is, I love being with people when the lightning strikes. I'll stop right there and acknowledge it. I'll talk about how significant those words are and how big of a breakthrough it is. I try to write them on the board where everyone can see it. Usually at the end of a workshop, I've got a few statements written down like that.

When you stop and honor someone's words, when you acknowledge their importance, you acknowledge their gravitas. Gravitas comes from a Latin word that means "weight" (think gravity). It's about credibility and respect. When you point out that gravitas, you give them your respect by honoring their words. As the listener, you also have gravitas. You give them the weight of your attention and emotions when you honor their words.

One of my favorite phrases is "I love the way you said that." Remember, I'm a truth teller, and you can't fake this kind of stuff. You have to be real, transparent, authentic. It doesn't work if you're not.

When you stop and marvel at what someone just said, you're lending them your spotlight for just a few moments and telling them they did a good thing. It's powerful to recognize their words.

BIG FEELINGS

Emotions stir up something within us, often things that don't come to the surface very often. For example, the feelings that precede tears come from the deep. Stop there for a moment and respect those displays of emotions. When they get vulnerable, acknowledge the moment and the emotions. Hang out there and tread lightly.

Ask about it. Acknowledge it in some way. Say something like, "Man, that seemed to really hit home." Maybe it's just "That sounds hard." If you don't do this, it'll seem as if you missed it, didn't care, or were distracted, and none of those are good.

These big feelings are places where real connection is waiting, and people want you there with them. People want to be seen and heard. If you see their feelings but don't respond to them, it sends a powerful message. People notice when you notice. Stop, take the time—as long as it takes.

Lean in when you hear significant words like *cancer, abortion, divorce, death, suicide,* or anything close. You get the idea. Never gloss over or forget the psychological toll of their big words, even if they're referencing something from years ago. Stop and acknowledge their feelings.

Conversational trends will help you identify these big feelings. I know someone who lost a loved one, and often in our conversation, this will come up. They usually say something like, "When I lost my brother . . .

Don't underestimate the emotions someone is feeling or expressing during your conversations, even if you don't understand them. You may struggle to empathize because you haven't been through a similar experience. Just acknowledge their reality.

As we close this chapter on emotions, never forget how powerful they are. When properly acknowledged, they create strong connective tissue between people.

CONCLUSION

You Got This!

—ɯ—

The most difficult thing is the decision to act; the rest is merely tenacity.
—Amelia Earhart

IF YOU'VE MADE IT THIS far, you have everything you need to have a great conversation. You're on your way to deeper connection. These are skills that can be improved with intentionality, a little effort, and a few easy-to-use tools.

Key concepts and tools

- Listen in high gear and head for the deep end of the pool. (Chapter 8)
- Suspend judgment: don't cross the Bridge of Decision. (Chapter 3)
- 80/20: listen 80 percent, speak 20 percent. (Chapter 3)
- Listen on all levels, with your ears and your eyes. (Chapter 5)
- Don't multitask: focus completely on the other person. (Chapter 4)
- The Art of the Pause: think about what to say, then speak. (Chapter 2)
- The Art of the Follow-Up Question: "Tell me more about that." (Chapter 7)
- The Dynamic Duo of Reflection and Inquiry: repeat their words, then dig in with a question about those words. (Chapter 6)

In all these things, be genuine. If you use these tools to manipulate, it'll be obvious. Being inauthentic is worse than showing no interest at all.

GET SOME REPS.

Now it's time to put these steps into action. Start with a low-stress situation. Try a few things out, and see how it goes. When your heart is in it, you'll see success. Remember the story about travelers in other countries trying to speak the language? People will recognize and reward your effort.

If your heart isn't in it but you want it to be, you'll see success there as well. Remember that feelings follow action; the action jump-starts the feelings. "Tell me more about that" encompasses many of the key concepts. It's an easy go-to that works most of the time.

The life that matters is the one unfolding right here, right now.

Remind yourself where you want to be. All you need is a genuine mustard seed of desire and a bit of helpful advice to get started. It's not that hard. When they see your honest effort, you'll win them over. Try it in the line at the grocery store, or anywhere you find yourself standing with someone. Once you're comfortable with the basics, move into next-level conversations in other social situations.

Core message: make it about them.

Let that be your takeaway. *Make it about them.* That, along with the other tools you've seen here, will win the day for you. Give it a go! I think you'll be pleasantly surprised.

Author Biography

Keith Allbritten is a Fortune 500 leadership coach and former US Air Force aviator with a lifelong passion for helping people make authentic connections. Over the course of his career, he's trained leaders, mentored professionals, and guided countless conversations. Known for his engaging storytelling and down-to-earth approach, Keith brings together lessons from the cockpit, the boardroom, and the  coffee shop. His mission is simple: to guide people out of the shallow end of chatter and into the deep end of meaningful conversation. *Talk Like It Matters* is his first book.

www.ingramcontent.com/pod-product-compliance
Lightning Source LLC
Chambersburg PA
CBHW020500030426
42337CB00011B/174